A BALANCED MATHEMATICS PROGRAM INTEGRATING SCIENCE AND LANGUAGE ARTS

Unit Resource Guide
Unit 12
Exploring Fractions

THIRD EDITION

KENDALL/HUNT PUBLISHING COMPANY
4050 Westmark Drive   Dubuque, Iowa 52002

A TIMS® Curriculum
University of Illinois at Chicago

UIC The University of Illinois
at Chicago

The original edition was based on work supported by the National Science Foundation under grant No. MDR 9050226 and the University of Illinois at Chicago. Any opinions, findings, and conclusions or recommendations expressed in this publication are those of the author(s) and do not necessarily reflect the views of the granting agencies.

Letter Home

Exploring Fractions

Date: _____

Dear Family Member:

The activities in this unit will help your child better understand fractions. Your child will explore the concept of a whole. Understanding the size of the whole is important to understanding the fractional parts of that whole. For example, a half gallon of milk is larger than a half cup of milk because the whole is larger.

Another important idea is shown in the picture. The fewer pieces the pie is divided into, the larger each piece will be. Grace ate more pie than Jessie or Shannon—$\frac{2}{4}$ is greater than $\frac{2}{6}$ or $\frac{2}{12}$. Your child will use concrete models to name fractions, compare the size of fractions, and add and subtract fractions.

Shannon ate $\frac{2}{12}$ of an apple pie, Jessie ate $\frac{2}{6}$ of a peach pie, and Grace ate $\frac{2}{4}$ of a cherry pie. Who ate the most pie?

You can help your child understand fractions by pointing out places where fractions are used outside of school. Examples include preparing a recipe, measuring wood for a project, purchasing fabric, or advertising sales.

Continue the ongoing practice of the division facts. In this unit, students will practice and then take a quiz on the division facts for the nines. Use the *Triangle Flash Cards: 9s* to help your child practice these facts.

Thank you for your time and cooperation.

Sincerely,

_____

Carta al hogar

Explorando fracciones

Fecha: _____

Estimado miembro de familia:

Las actividades de esta unidad ayudarán a su hijo/a a entender mejor las fracciones. Su hijo/a explorará el concepto de entero. Comprender el tamaño de un entero es importante para comprender las partes fraccionales de un entero. Por ejemplo, medio galón de leche es más que media taza de leche porque el entero es más grande.

En el dibujo se muestra otra idea importante. En cuantas menos porciones se divide el pastel, más grande será cada porción. Grace comió más pastel que Jessie o Shannon: $\frac{2}{4}$ es más grande que $\frac{2}{6}$ ó $\frac{2}{12}$. Su hijo/a usará modelos concretos para nombrar fracciones, comparar el tamaño de fracciones, y sumar y restar fracciones.

Shannon comió $\frac{2}{12}$ de un pastel de manzana, Jessie comió $\frac{2}{6}$ de un pastel de durazno, y Grace comió $\frac{2}{4}$ de un pastel de cereza. ¿Quién comió más pastel?

Usted puede ayudar a su hijo/a a entender el concepto de fracciones señalando lugares donde se usan fracciones fuera de la escuela. Los ejemplos incluyen preparar una receta, medir madera para un proyecto, comprar tela o publicidad de ofertas.

Continúe practicando las tablas de división. En esta unidad, los estudiantes practicarán y luego tomarán un examen sobre las tablas de división del nueve. Use las tarjetas triangulares para ayudar a su hijo/a a practicar estas divisiones.

Gracias por su tiempo y su cooperación.

Atentamente,

_____

Table of Contents

Unit 12
Exploring Fractions

Unit 12

Outline
Exploring Fractions

Unit Summary

Through the use of manipulatives, students continue to build a strong conceptual understanding of fractions. Students explore part-whole fractions with fraction strips and pattern blocks. They use manipulatives to compare and order fractions as well as add and subtract fractions with like denominators. An open-response problem involving fraction pattern block puzzles, *Puzzle Problem,* is included as an assessment lesson. This unit also includes a midterm test that covers concepts from this and past units. The DPP reviews and assesses the division facts for the nines.

Major Concept Focus

- writing fractions
- modeling fractions with manipulatives
- equivalent fractions
- communicating problem-solving strategies
- ordering fractions
- fractions in measurement
- part-whole fractions
- Student Rubrics: *Solving* and *Telling*
- midterm test
- adding and subtracting fractions with manipulatives
- adding and subtracting fractions with like denominators
- division facts for the nines

Pacing Suggestions

- Lesson 4 *Frabble Game and Bubble Sort* is an optional lesson. These activities provide opportunities to practice and extend fraction concepts in game situations.
- Lesson 6 *Pattern Block Fractions* contains an optional activity from third grade that introduces students to using pattern blocks to represent fractions. Use it with students who have not had these experiences.

Assessment Indicators

Use the following Assessment Indicators and the *Observational Assessment Record* that follows the Background section in this unit to assess students on key ideas.

A1. Can students represent fractions using pattern blocks and paper folding?

A2. Can students identify the whole when given a fractional part of the whole?

A3. Can students find equivalent fractions using manipulatives?

A4. Can students compare and order fractions using manipulatives?

A5. Can students add and subtract fractions with like denominators using manipulatives?

A6. Can students solve open-response problems and communicate solution strategies?

A7. Do students demonstrate fluency with the division facts for the 9s?

Unit Planner

KEY: SG = Student Guide, DAB = Discovery Assignment Book, AB = Adventure Book, URG = Unit Resource Guide, DPP = Daily Practice and Problems, HP = Home Practice (found in Discovery Assignment Book), and TIG = Teacher Implementation Guide.

	Lesson Information	Supplies	Copies/Transparencies
Lesson 1 **Fraction Strips** URG Pages 28–47 SG Pages 326–332 DAB Pages 199–201 DPP A–F HP Parts 1–2 *Estimated Class Sessions* **3**	**Activity** Students fold uniform strips of paper to show equal parts, labeling each part according to the fractional part it represents. Students will fold halves, thirds, fourths, fifths, sixths, eighths, ninths, tenths, and twelfths. Students will then use the strips to find equivalent fractions. **Math Facts** DPP items B and C and Home Practice Part 1 review and provide practice with the division facts for the nines. **Homework** 1. Assign homework *Questions 1–7* in the *Student Guide* any time after Part 1, homework *Questions 8–13* after Part 2, and homework *Questions 14–21* after Part 3. 2. Students take their flash cards home to study the division facts for the nines. 3. Assign Home Practice Part 2 in the *Discovery Assignment Book*. **Assessment** Use the *Observational Assessment Record* to record students' abilities to represent fractions with paper folding.	• 1 pair of scissors per student • 2 envelopes per student (1 for flash cards and 1 for fraction strips) • crayons, markers, or colored pencils • 1 ruler per student	• 1 copy of *Fraction Strips for the Teacher* URG Pages 42–43 • 1 copy of *Observational Assessment Record* URG Pages 13–14 to be used throughout this unit
Lesson 2 **Adding and Subtracting with Fraction Strips** URG Pages 48–53 SG Pages 333–335 DPP G–H *Estimated Class Sessions* **1**	**Activity** Students use fraction strips to add and subtract fractions with like denominators. **Math Facts** DPP Bit G provides practice with division facts and Task H provides practice with prime factorization. **Homework** Assign homework *Questions 1–7* in the *Student Guide*. Students will need their fraction strips. **Assessment** Use the *Observational Assessment Record* to note students' progress adding and subtracting fractions with like denominators using manipulatives.	• 1 set of fraction strips from Lesson 1 per student	• 1 set of cut strips, folded, colored, and labeled copied from *Fraction Strips for the Teacher* URG Pages 42–43
Lesson 3 **Comparing Fractions** URG Pages 54–63 SG Pages 336–338 DPP I–J *Estimated Class Sessions* **1**	**Activity** Students organize their fraction strips in a chart and then use the chart to compare and order fractions according to size. **Homework** Assign homework *Questions 1–8* in the *Student Guide*. **Assessment** Use the *Observational Assessment Record* to note students' abilities to order fractions.	• glue • 1 sheet of blank paper per student • 1 set of fraction strips from Lesson 1 per student	• 1 copy of *Fraction Strips for the Teacher* URG Pages 42–43 • 1 transparency of *Fraction Chart* URG Page 61

	Lesson Information	Supplies	Copies/Transparencies
Lesson 4 **Frabble Game and Bubble Sort** URG Pages 64–70 SG Pages 339–342 DAB Pages 203–209 *Estimated Class Sessions* **1-2**	OPTIONAL LESSON **Optional Game** Students use a deck of fraction cards to complete two activities. First, students play a game in small groups in which they order fractions according to size by strategically placing cards on the table. Then in an activity called Bubble Sort, each student holds a fraction card as he or she stands in line. Following simple rules, they rearrange themselves so the cards are in order. **Homework** Students play *Frabble* at home. They should take home a deck of *Frabble* cards, six wild cards, and their *Student Guides*. **Assessment** Use the *Observational Assessment Record* to note students' abilities to compare and order fractions.	• 1 pair of scissors per student • envelopes, optional • 1 fraction chart from Lesson 3 per student	• 1 transparency of *Standard Frabble Cards* DAB Pages 203–205, optional • 1 transparency of *Fraction Chart* URG Page 61 or fraction chart from Lesson 3
Lesson 5 **Equivalent Fractions** URG Pages 71–79 SG Pages 343–345 DPP K–L HP Part 3 *Estimated Class Sessions* **1**	**Activity** Students find equivalent fractions using their fraction charts from Lesson 3, write number sentences to represent the fractions, and look for patterns in the number sentences. They use the patterns to write an equivalent fraction for a given fraction. **Math Facts** Use DPP items K and L to practice multiplication and division facts as students build number sense. **Homework** Assign the Homework section on the *Equivalent Fractions* Activity Pages in the *Student Guide*. Students will need their fraction charts to complete this assignment. **Assessment** 1. Use the *Observational Assessment Record* to note students' abilities to find equivalent fractions. 2. Use Home Practice Part 3 as an assessment.	• 1 fraction chart from Lesson 3 per student	

(Continued)

	Lesson Information	Supplies	Copies/Transparencies

Lesson 6

Pattern Block Fractions

URG Pages 80–95
SG Pages 346–349

DPP M–P
HP Parts 4–5

Estimated Class Sessions
2-3

Activity
Students explore the use of pattern blocks to model fractions. They name fractions when a given pattern block is defined as one whole, and they identify the whole when a fraction is given. They also model easy addition problems using pattern blocks.

Math Facts
DPP Bit M provides practice with math facts. Item P focuses on different aspects of division.

Homework
1. Assign *Questions 1–7* in the Homework section of the *Student Guide*. These questions review skills and concepts addressed in Lessons 1–5.
2. Assign Home Practice Parts 4 and 5.
3. Students continue practicing division facts using the *Triangle Flash Cards: 9s.*

Assessment
Use the *Observational Assessment Record* to note students' abilities to identify the whole when given a fractional part of the whole.

- 1 set of pattern blocks (2–3 yellow hexagons, 6 red trapezoids, 10 blue rhombuses, 10 green triangles, 6 brown trapezoids) per student pair
- overhead pattern blocks, optional

- 1 copy of *What's 1?* URG Pages 88–89 per student, optional

Lesson 7

Solving Problems with Pattern Blocks

URG Pages 96–103
SG Pages 350–352

DPP Q–R

Estimated Class Sessions
1

Activity
Students use pattern blocks to order fractions by looking at patterns. They develop a strategy for ordering fractions. They also solve word problems involving addition of fractions using pattern blocks.

Homework
Assign *Questions 1–5* in the Homework section in the *Student Guide.*

Assessment
Use DPP items Q and R as assessments.

- 1 set of pattern blocks (2–3 yellow hexagons, 6 red trapezoids, 10 blue rhombuses, 10 green triangles, 6 brown trapezoids) per student pair
- 1 fraction chart from Lesson 3 per student pair
- overhead pattern blocks, optional

Lesson 8

Fraction Puzzles

URG Pages 104–117
SG Pages 353–355

DPP S–V
HP Part 6

Estimated Class Sessions
2

Assessment Activity
Students work cooperatively in groups of four to solve fraction puzzles. Four clues are given to help the groups solve each puzzle. After finding a solution, students write a paragraph explaining their solutions and the problem-solving strategies used by their groups.

Homework
1. Assign homework *Questions 1–7* in the *Student Guide.*
2. Assign Home Practice Part 6.

- 1 set of pattern blocks per student group
- envelopes, optional
- paper clips, optional

- 1 copy of *Fraction Puzzle Clues* URG Pages 112–113 per student group
- 1 copy of *Puzzle Problem* URG Page 114 per student
- 1 transparency or poster of Student Rubric: *Solving* TIG, Assessment section
- 1 transparency or poster of Student Rubric: *Telling* TIG, Assessment section

Lesson Information	Supplies	Copies/Transparencies
Assessment 1. Puzzle D and the *Puzzle Problem* Assessment Blackline Master provide an assessment of students' problem-solving and communication skills. 2. Use the *Observational Assessment Record* to note students' abilities to solve open-response problems and communicate solution strategies. 3. Transfer appropriate documentation from the Unit 12 *Observational Assessment Record* to students' *Individual Assessment Record Sheets.*		• 1 copy of *TIMS Multidimensional Rubric* TIG, Assessment section • 1 copy of *Individual Assessment Record Sheet* TIG Assessment section per student, previously copied for use throughout the year
Lesson 9 **Midterm Test** URG Pages 118–129 DPP W–X *Estimated Class Sessions* **1-2** **Assessment Activity** Students take a test on concepts in this and past units. **Math Facts** DPP Bit W is a short quiz on division facts.	• 1 calculator per student • 1 ruler per student • 1 protractor per student • base-ten pieces • pattern blocks • 1 fraction chart from Lesson 3 per student	• 1 copy of *Midterm Test* URG Pages 122–126 per student

A current list of literature and software connections is available at *www.mathtrailblazers.com.* You can also find information on connections in the *Teacher Implementation Guide* Literature List and Software List sections.

Literature Connections

Suggested Titles

- Adler, David A. *Fraction Fun.* Holiday House, New York, 1997.
- Pallotta, Jerry. *Hershey's Fraction Book.* Cartwheel Press, New York, 1999.
- Stamper, Judith Bauer. *Go Fractions.* Grosset and Dunlap, New York, 2003.

Software Connections

- *Fraction Attraction* develops understanding of fractions using fraction bars, pie charts, hundreds blocks, and other materials.
- *Math Arena* is a collection of math activities that reinforces many math concepts.
- *Math Munchers Deluxe* provides practice with equivalent fractions and other skills in an arcade-like game.
- *Math Mysteries: Fractions* develops multistep problem solving with fractions.
- *Math Workshop Deluxe* allows students to explore fractions and decimals.
- *Mighty Math Number Heroes* poses short answer questions about fractions and other number operations.
- *National Library of Virtual Manipulatives* website (http://matti.usu.edu) allows students to work with fractions using pattern blocks and other manipulatives on the computer.
- *Tenth Planet: Fraction Operation* develops conceptual understanding of fraction operations.
- *Tenth Planet: Representing Fractions* provides a conceptual introduction to fractions.

Teaching All Math Trailblazers Students

Math Trailblazers® lessons are designed for students with a wide range of abilities. The lessons are flexible and do not require significant adaptation for diverse learning styles or academic levels. However, when needed, lessons can be tailored to allow students to engage their abilities to the greatest extent possible while building knowledge and skills.

To assist you in meeting the needs of all students in your classroom, this section contains information about some of the features in the curriculum that allow all students access to mathematics. For additional information, see the Teaching the *Math Trailblazers* Student: Meeting Individual Needs section in the *Teacher Implementation Guide.*

Differentiation Opportunities in this Unit

Games

Use games to promote or extend understanding of math concepts and to practice skills with children who need more practice.

- *Frabble Game* from Lesson 4 *Frabble Game and Bubble Sort*

Journal Prompts

Journal prompts provide opportunities for students to explain and reflect on mathematical problems. They can help both students who need practice explaining their ideas and students who benefit from answering higher order questions. Students with various learning styles can express themselves using pictures, words, and sentences. Teachers can alter journal prompts to suit students' ability levels. The following lessons contain a journal prompt:

- Lesson 2 *Adding and Subtracting with Fraction Strips*
- Lesson 3 *Comparing Fractions*
- Lesson 6 *Pattern Block Fractions*
- Lesson 7 *Solving Problems with Pattern Blocks*

DPP Challenges

DPP Challenges are items from the Daily Practice and Problems that usually take more than fifteen minutes to complete. These problems are more thought-provoking and can be used to stretch students' problem-solving skills. The following lessons have DPP Challenges in them:

- DPP Challenge N from Lesson 6 *Pattern Block Fractions*
- DPP Challenges T and V from Lesson 8 *Fraction Puzzles*

Extensions

Use extensions to enrich lessons. Many extensions provide opportunities to further involve or challenge students of all abilities. Take a moment to review the extensions prior to beginning this unit. Some extensions may require additional preparation and planning. The following lessons contain extensions:

- Lesson 4 *Frabble Game and Bubble Sort*
- Lesson 6 *Pattern Block Fractions*
- Lesson 8 *Fraction Puzzles*

Background
Exploring Fractions

Throughout the *Math Trailblazers* curriculum, students have used manipulatives to explore fractions. In this unit, students continue to build a strong conceptual understanding of fractions through the use of manipulatives.

Most fractions we encounter fall into one of the following contexts:

- part-whole fractions
- indicated divisions
- ratios
- measurements
- names of points on a number line
- pure numbers
- probabilities

In this unit, part-whole fractions are the main focus, but fractions of measurements are also included. Other units within the curriculum will focus on other types of fractions.

Learning about fractions is often difficult for children. This difficulty is understandable considering the complexity of the concepts involved. The fact that many children misunderstand fractions is illustrated by the results of the National Assessment of Educational Progress (Kouba, et al., 1988). In this assessment, many 9-, 13-, and 17-year-olds were shown to lack proficiency in working with fractions. Students appeared to have done their computations mechanically with little understanding of the underlying fraction concepts (National Research Council, 2001).

When students begin to study fractions, they usually have a good understanding of the system of whole numbers. Unless students develop a conceptual understanding of fractions, this understanding of whole number concepts often interferes with their abilities to learn fraction concepts. The following represent some of the roadblocks students may experience if they do not develop a conceptual understanding of fractions.

1. Consider the symbol $\frac{3}{4}$. This number is made up of two parts, the numerator and the denominator, each represented by a whole number with a specific meaning or value. The denominator tells us that the whole is divided into 4 equal parts, and the numerator tells us that we are concerned with 3 of these parts. In addition to understanding these two values, a student must understand that the symbol $\frac{3}{4}$ also represents a single number with a unique value.

2. Students learn in the whole number system that 4 is less than 6. However, when comparing the fractions $\frac{1}{4}$ and $\frac{1}{6}$, $\frac{1}{4}$ is larger than $\frac{1}{6}$. Students may have difficulty with the inverse relationship between the number of parts into which the whole is divided and the size of these parts. That is, the more parts a whole is divided into, the smaller each part is. The following exchange between a teacher and student illustrates this confusion (Post, et al., 1985):

Teacher: One-fifth and one-ninth—which is less?

Student: One-fifth is less, because five is less than nine.

[The teacher directs the student to use colored parts to illustrate.]

Student: [Covers one circular unit with orange ($\frac{1}{5}$) parts and another with white ($\frac{1}{9}$) parts, as shown in Figure 1.] It takes 9 white and 5 orange.

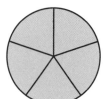

Figure 1: *Two fraction circles illustrating fifths and ninths*

Teacher: [Draws attention to colored parts] Which is less, one-fifth or one-ninth?

Student: One-fifth, because it takes five to cover this, and it takes nine to cover this [points to the circular units].

Student: One orange is bigger than one white. One-fifth is less than one-ninth.

3. The previous vignette also illustrates the difficulty many students have with the language we use as we teach fractions. This language may not be clearly understood by all students. For example when we ask, "Which fraction is less?" do we mean which is less in size or do we mean which needs a lesser amount to cover the whole? Likewise, when asking, "Which is greater?" are we asking which fraction covers a greater area of the whole or which fraction results in a greater number of parts?

4. As students begin to compare and order fractions, their understanding of the whole number system is further challenged. When students order fractions with like denominators, they use the numerators to order the fractions. Ordering fractions using the numerator has a direct relationship to the whole number system. That is, $\frac{1}{4} < \frac{2}{4} < \frac{3}{4} < \frac{4}{4}$. However, when students compare and order fractions with like numerators, this relationship changes. Students use the denominators to order fractions, finding that $\frac{2}{9} < \frac{2}{5} < \frac{2}{3}$. When both the numerators and denominators are different, students must have a solid understanding of fractions so that they can choose efficient and flexible strategies to compare the fractions.

5. Students can also become confused with counting issues when working with fractions. For example, when you count using whole numbers, you know that 1 comes before 2 and 3 comes after 2. However, when counting with fractions it is difficult to know what comes next. For example, what fraction follows $\frac{1}{2}$ on the number line?

Each roadblock can affect a child's understanding of fractions and subsequent ability to use them correctly. Students need classroom experiences to help them develop a strong conceptual understanding of fractions. The use of manipulatives is crucial in developing this understanding. Research shows that students who learn with the help of manipulatives generally score higher on achievement tests than students whose instruction includes no use of manipulatives. (Suydam, 1986) Emphasize the use of manipulatives in the classroom to help students construct fraction meaning as they explore fraction concepts. Furthermore, have students use more than one type of manipulative as they explore fractions. This increases the likelihood that they will generalize their understandings beyond the tangible (the manipulatives) to the symbolic representation. In this unit, we use both paper folding and pattern blocks to help students develop a strong mental image of fractions. Students use both these physical models to name fractions and to represent fractions when given a fraction value.

We explore the concept of a unit or a whole using pattern blocks. We ask students to find the value of different blocks based on the defined whole. For example, when a yellow hexagon is defined as one whole, the blue rhombus equals $\frac{1}{3}$ of the whole. However, when a red trapezoid is defined as one whole, the green triangle equals $\frac{1}{3}$. Students develop the understanding that the size of the fraction depends on the size of the whole.

Students explore equivalent fractions using both paper folding and pattern blocks. Students also compare fractions using both manipulatives. They compare fractions with like denominators and like numerators and are encouraged to develop a strategy for ordering fractions with like numerators.

Finally, we introduce students to simple addition and subtraction of fractions using manipulatives and to the symbolic representation of these problems. However, they are only expected to solve problems in which the symbolic representations are paired with physical models.

Resources

- Cramer, K., T. Post, and R. del Mas. "Initial Fraction Learning by Fourth- and Fifth-Grade Students: A Comparison of the Effects of Using Commercial Curricula with the Effects of Using the Rational Number Project Curriculum." *Journal for Research in Mathematics Education,* 33 (2), pp. 111–144, March 2002.

- Curcio, Frances R. (series editor). *Curriculum and Evaluation Standards for School Mathematics, Addenda Series 5–8: Understanding Rational Numbers and Proportions.* National Council of Teachers of Mathematics, Reston, VA, 1994.

- Driscoll, Mark J. *Research Within Reach, Elementary School Mathematics.* National Council of Teachers of Mathematics, Reston, VA, 1986.

- Kouba, et al. "Result of the Fourth NAEP Assessment of Mathematics: Number, Operations, and Word Problems." *Arithmetic Teacher,* 35 (8), April 1988.

- National Research Council. *Adding It Up: Helping Children Learn Mathematics.* J. Kilpatrick, J. Swafford, and B. Findell, Eds. Mathematics Learning Study Committee, Center for Education, Division of Behavioral and Social Sciences and Education, National Academy Press, Washington, DC, 2001.

- Post, Thomas, Ipke Wachsmuth, Richard Lesh, Merlyn Behr. "Order and Equivalence of Rational Numbers: A Cognitive Analysis." *Journal for Research in Mathematics Education,* 16 (1), January 1985.

- Post, Thomas R. (editor). *Teaching Mathematics in Grades K–8, Research Based Methods.* Allyn and Bacon, Boston, 1992.

- Suydam, Marilyn. "Manipulatives, Materials and Achievement." *Arithmetic Teacher,* 33 (6), February 1986.

- Trafton, Paul, and Albert P. Shulte, (editors). *New Directions for Elementary School Mathematics, 1989 Yearbook.* National Council of Teachers of Mathematics, Reston, VA, 1989.

Observational Assessment Record

A1 Can students represent fractions using pattern blocks and paper folding?

A2 Can students identify the whole when given a fractional part of the whole?

A3 Can students find equivalent fractions using manipulatives?

A4 Can students compare and order fractions using manipulatives?

A5 Can students add and subtract fractions with like denominators using manipulatives?

A6 Can students solve open-response problems and communicate solution strategies?

A7 Do students demonstrate fluency with the division facts for the 9s?

A8 _____

Name	A1	A2	A3	A4	A5	A6	A7	A8	Comments
1.									
2.									
3.									
4.									
5.									
6.									
7.									
8.									
9.									
10.									
11.									
12.									
13.									

Name	A1	A2	A3	A4	A5	A6	A7	A8	Comments
14.									
15.									
16.									
17.									
18.									
19.									
20.									
21.									
22.									
23.									
24.									
25.									
26.									
27.									
28.									
29.									
30.									
31.									
32.									

Unit 12

Daily Practice and Problems
Exploring Fractions

A DPP Menu for Unit 12

Two Daily Practice and Problems (DPP) items are included for each class session listed in the Unit Outline. A scope and sequence chart for the DPP is in the *Teacher Implementation Guide*.

Icons in the Teacher Notes column designate the subject matter of each DPP item. The first item in each class session is always a Bit and the second is either a Task or Challenge. Each item falls into one or more of the categories listed below. A menu of the DPP items for Unit 12 follows.

N Number Sense	Computation	Time	Geometry
E, H–J, O, Q–V	D, J–L, P	A, F	N, X

Math Facts	$ Money	Measurement	Data
B, C, G, H, K–M, P, W	F, V	N, X	

Practice and Assessment of the Division Facts

The DPP for this unit continues the systematic strategies-based approach to learning the division facts. This unit provides practice and assessment for the nines. The *Triangle Flash Cards: 9s* may be found in the *Discovery Assignment Book* following the Home Practice and in the *Grade 4 Facts*

Resource Guide. A discussion of the flash cards and how they might be used is in item B of the DPP. A quiz on these facts is in item W.

For more information about the distribution and assessment of the math facts, see the TIMS Tutor: *Math Facts* in the *Teacher Implementation Guide* and the *Grade 4 Facts Resource Guide.* Also refer to the DPP guides in the *Unit Resource Guide* for Units 3 and 9.

Students may solve the items individually, in groups, or as a class. The items may also be assigned for homework. The DPPs are also available on the Teacher Resource CD.

Student Questions	Teacher Notes

A. Telling Time

How much time has passed from:

A. 12:10 to 12:30?

B. 1:45 to 2:05?

C. 3:20 to 4:00?

D. 5:25 to 5:55?

E. 11:10 to 12:25?

TIMS Bit

A. 20 minutes

B. 20 minutes

C. 40 minutes

D. 30 minutes

E. 1 hour and 15 minutes

Division Facts: 9s

TIMS Task

With a partner, use your *Triangle Flash Cards: 9s* to quiz each other on the division facts for the nines. Ask your partner first to cover the numbers in the squares. Use the two uncovered numbers to solve a division fact. Separate the flash cards into three piles: those facts you know and can answer quickly, those you can figure out with a strategy, and those you need to learn.

Then go through the cards again and have your partner cover the numbers in the circles. Use the uncovered numbers to solve a division fact. Separate the cards into three piles again.

Both times through, practice the facts that are in the last two piles and make a list of these facts so you can practice them at home.

Circle all the facts you know and can answer quickly on your *Division Facts I Know* chart.

Repeat this process for your partner.

The *Triangle Flash Cards: 9s* are located after the Home Practice in the *Discovery Assignment Book*. Blackline masters of all the flash cards, organized by group, are in the *Grade 4 Facts Resource Guide*. Part 1 of the Home Practice reminds students to take home the list of facts they need to study as well as their flash cards.

Inform students when you will give the quiz on the nines. This quiz appears in TIMS Bit W.

C Division Facts

A. $81 \div 9 =$ B. $9 \div 9 =$

C. $63 \div 9 =$ D. $27 \div 9 =$

E. $36 \div 9 =$ F. $54 \div 9 =$

G. $18 \div 9 =$ H. $72 \div 9 =$

I. $9 \div 1 =$ J. $45 \div 9 =$

TIMS Bit

A. 9	B. 1
C. 7	D. 3
E. 4	F. 6
G. 2	H. 8
I. 9	J. 5

D Multiplication

Use paper and pencil or mental math to solve the following problems. Estimate to make sure your answers are reasonable.

1. A. $53 \times 4 =$ B. $459 \times 4 =$

    C. $5532 \times 4 =$ D. $26 \times 45 =$

    E. $22 \times 7 =$ F. $724 \times 3 =$

    G. $3096 \times 5 =$ H. $38 \times 52 =$

2. Explain your strategy for Question 1A.

3. Explain your estimation strategy for Question 1D.

TIMS Task

1. A. 212	B. 1836
C. 22,128	D. 1170
E. 154	F. 2172
G. 15,480	H. 1976

2. Possible mental math strategy:
   $4 \times 50 = 200$;
   $4 \times 3 = 12$;
   $200 + 12 = 212$.

3. Possible strategy:
   Round 26 up to 30;
   round 45 down to 40;
   $30 \times 40 = 1200$.

E Decimals in Sequence

Write the next 3 decimals:

A. 1.0   1.5   2.0   2.5   3.0   ___ ___ ___

B. 6.4   6.8   7.2   7.6   8.0   ___ ___ ___

C. 2.2   3.2   4.2   5.2   6.2   ___ ___ ___

TIMS Bit

A. 3.5, 4.0, 4.5

B. 8.4, 8.8, 9.2

C. 7.2, 8.2, 9.2

F **Earning an Allowance**

Irma's aunt pays her 5 cents for each minute she reads a book instead of watching television. She began reading at 4:48 and finished at 5:19. How much money did she make? Tell the strategies you used to get your answer.

TIMS Task

$1.55

G **More Division Facts**

Find the number *n* that makes the sentence true.

A. $72 \div 8 = n$ B. $n \div 9 = 6$

C. $n \div 9 = 5$ D. $36 \div 4 = n$

E. $27 \div n = 9$ F. $n \div 9 = 9$

G. $n \div 9 = 2$ H. $63 \div n = 9$

TIMS Bit

A. 9   B. 54

C. 45   D. 9

E. 3   F. 81

G. 18   H. 7

H **Prime Factors**

1. Which of the following are prime numbers?

53   54   57   67   96   103

2. For the composite numbers, use factor trees to factor them into a product of primes. You may use a calculator.

TIMS Task

1. 53, 67, 103

2.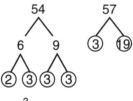

$3^3 \times 2$ 3×19

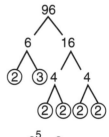

$2^5 \times 3$

Decimals from Pictures

Write a decimal for the shaded part of each picture. The flat is one whole.

1.
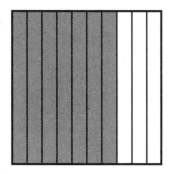

2.
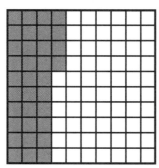

3.
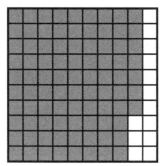

4.
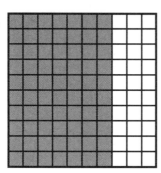

TIMS Bit

1. 0.7   2. 0.34

3. 0.87   4. 0.70 or 0.7

J **More Multiplication**

1. Solve the following using a paper-and-pencil method.

   A. $239 \times 7 =$ B. $3729 \times 3 =$

   C. $2390 \times 2 =$ D. $79 \times 23 =$

2. Find at least two ways to round each of the answers to Questions 1A through 1D.

TIMS Task

1. A. 1673
   B. 11,187
   C. 4780
   D. 1817

Answers will vary for Question 2.
Possible answers are given below.

2. A. 2000; 1700
   B. 11,000; 11,200
   C. 5000; 4800
   D. 2000; 1800

Student Questions	Teacher Notes

 More Division Fact Practice

Find the number *n* that makes each sentence true.

A. $54 \div n = 9$

B. $720 \div n = 90$

C. $n \times 400 = 36{,}000$

D. $70 \times n = 63{,}000$

E. $90 \times n = 450$

F. $n \div 9 = 300$

TIMS Bit

A. 6

B. 8

C. 90

D. 900

E. 5

F. 2700

 Fact Practice

A. $30 \times 90 =$

B. $630 \div 70 =$

C. $360 \div 9 =$

D. $90 \times 80 =$

E. $2700 \div 9 =$

F. $9000 \times 90 =$

G. $54{,}000 \div 9 =$

H. $1800 \div 90 =$

I. $900 \times 0 =$

J. $900 \div 90 =$

TIMS Task

A. 2700

B. 9

C. 40

D. 7200

E. 300

F. 810,000

G. 6000

H. 20

I. 0

J. 10

Fact Families for × and ÷

Solve the given fact. Then name another fact in the same fact family.

A. $9 \times 8 =$

B. $54 \div 9 =$

C. $36 \div 4 =$

D. $9 \times 7 =$

TIMS Bit

Complete this item orally as a class. Have one student solve the given fact and another student name a related fact. The answers and possible related facts are:

A. 72; 72 ÷ 9 = 8

B. 6; 6 × 9 = 54

C. 9; 4 × 9 = 36

D. 63; 63 ÷ 7 = 9

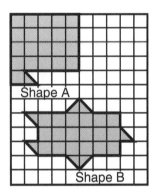

N **Area**

1. Draw two different shapes on *Centimeter Grid Paper.* Each shape should have an area of 21.5 square centimeters.

2. Measure the perimeter of your two shapes to the nearest tenth of a centimeter. Are the perimeters the same or different?

TIMS Challenge

1. Two sample shapes are shown below.

2. Perimeter of Shape A is 21.4 cm. Perimeter of Shape B is 23.8 cm. Be aware that lines on the diagonal are longer than 1 cm.

Student Questions	**Teacher Notes**

 Evenly Divisible

Frank wants to buy stickers for his 6 friends who will be attending his birthday party. At the store, he sees four different collections of stickers.

    One pad has 95 stickers.
    One pad has 110 stickers.
    One pad has 120 stickers.
    One pad has 160 stickers.

Frank plans to buy one pad of stickers. If he wants to divide the stickers evenly among his 6 guests without any leftovers, which pad should he purchase? How did you decide?

TIMS Bit

120 is divisible by 2 (it is even) and by 3 (the sum of the digits in 120 is a multiple of 3). Since 120 is divisible by 2 and 3, it is divisible by 6. Encourage students to share their strategies. Calculators should be available.

 Division Stories

Write a division story for 28 ÷ 9. Draw a picture for your story and write a number sentence that describes it. In your story, explain any remainder.

TIMS Task

Stories and pictures will vary. Students should label their pictures with the number sentence.

28 ÷ 9 = 3 R1 or
3 × 9 + 1 = 28

 Confused!

On planet Zimbo, a Zimbonese was told that the number 6 is larger than the number 4. But now there is confusion because the Zimbonese was also told that $\frac{1}{6}$ is smaller than $\frac{1}{4}$. Please use a diagram to explain why $\frac{1}{6}$ is smaller than $\frac{1}{4}$.

TIMS Bit

Possible diagram:

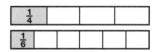

Be sure that the whole is the same for both fractions so when divided into six pieces, a one-sixth piece will be smaller than a piece from a whole divided into four pieces.

R **Further Confusion**

Brandon and Lee Yah invited the Zimbonese to eat pizza with them. Brandon has $\frac{1}{8}$ of a pizza and it is bigger in size than Lee Yah's $\frac{1}{4}$ of a pizza. The Zimbonese thought it understood (see DPP Bit Q) that $\frac{1}{8}$ was smaller than $\frac{1}{4}$. What needs to be changed so that $\frac{1}{8}$ is less than $\frac{1}{4}$?

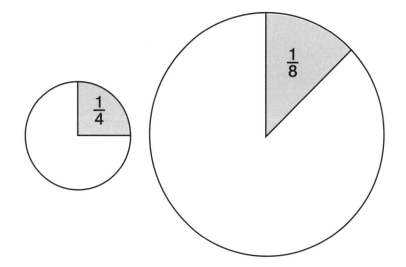

TIMS Task

The pizzas need to be the same size. Encourage students to write in their journals what they learned from the previous Bit and this Task.

S **Words to Numbers**

1. Write the following words as numbers.

   A. two-thirds   B. six-tenths

   C. five-eighths   D. one-twelfth

2. Write the following numbers as words.

   A. $\frac{3}{4}$ B. $\frac{7}{9}$

   C. $\frac{1}{2}$ D. $\frac{2}{5}$

TIMS Bit

1. A. $\frac{2}{3}$

   B. $\frac{6}{10}$ or 0.6

   C. $\frac{5}{8}$

   D. $\frac{1}{12}$

2. A. three-fourths

   B. seven-ninths

   C. one-half

   D. two-fifths

Art Paper

Carlos and Brandon each cut out a rectangle from a piece of drawing paper. Carlos's rectangle was larger—it was $\frac{1}{2}$ of his piece of paper. Brandon's was smaller, but it was $\frac{3}{4}$ of his whole piece.

1. Use *Centimeter Grid Paper* to draw a sketch of Brandon's and Carlos's whole pieces of paper.

2. Shade $\frac{1}{2}$ of Carlos's piece of paper.

3. Shade $\frac{3}{4}$ of Brandon's piece of paper.

TIMS Challenge

Accept all correct diagrams.

 Even Products

In your journal, explain why all multiples of 4 are even numbers. First, write all the multiples in order from 4 to 40.

TIMS Bit

4, 8, 12, 16, 20, 24, 28, 32, 36, 40

The multiples of 4 are even because a number divisible by 4 is also divisible by 2. Two is a factor of 4. All multiples of 2 are even.

Bank Deposit

The bank gives Maya wrappers so she can roll the coins she saves. Then she deposits the coins. The table shows the value of 1 roll of each type of coin.

Type of Coin	Value of 1 Roll
pennies	50¢
nickels	$2.00
dimes	$5.00
quarters	$10.00

Maya counts her change and puts the coins in wrappers. She has a total of $18.68. What types of coins could she have? How many full rolls of these coins could she have? How many coins would she have left over? List two possible combinations.

TIMS Challenge

Accept all possible answers. Two examples are listed below.

1 roll of quarters ($10) + 1 roll of dimes ($5) + 1 roll of nickels ($2) + 3 rolls of pennies ($.50 + $.50 + $.50) = $18.50 with 18¢ left over

or

3 rolls of dimes ($5 + $5 + $5) + 1 roll of nickels ($2) + 3 rolls of pennies ($.50 + $.50 + $.50) = $18.50 with 18¢ left over.

18¢ left over (18 pennies; 1 dime and 8 pennies; 1 dime, 1 nickel, and 3 pennies; 2 nickels and 8 pennies; 3 nickels and 3 pennies)

Student Questions	Teacher Notes

 Division Quiz: 9s

A. $72 \div 9 =$

B. $63 \div 9 =$

C. $54 \div 9 =$

D. $36 \div 9 =$

E. $81 \div 9 =$

F. $45 \div 9 =$

G. $9 \div 9 =$

H. $27 \div 9 =$

I. $18 \div 9 =$

TIMS Bit

A. 8 B. 7

C. 6 D. 4

E. 9 F. 5

G. 1 H. 3

I. 2

We recommend 1 minute for this quiz. Allow students to change pens after the time is up and complete the remaining problems in a different color. After students take the test, have them update their *Division Facts I Know* charts.

Since students learned the division facts through work with fact families, it is likely that the student who answers $72 \div 9$ correctly also knows the answer to $72 \div 8$. To make sure, however, after the quiz, ask students to write a related division fact for each fact on the quiz. A student who answers a given fact correctly and who also writes the correct related fact can circle both facts on the chart.

 Drawing Line Segments

Draw a 5-cm segment on your paper and label the endpoints E and G. Measure and mark the midpoint with the letter F. Extend the line 2 cm past E and label the new endpoint D. Now measure the length of $\overline{DF}$.

TIMS Task

2 cm   2.5 cm   2.5 cm

D   E   F   G

$\overline{DF}$ is 4.5 cm long.

Lesson 1

Fraction Strips

Lesson Overview

Students fold uniform strips of paper into equal parts, labeling each part according to the fraction it represents. Strips will be folded to show halves, thirds, fourths, fifths, sixths, eighths, ninths, tenths, and twelfths. Students will use their completed strips to show specific fractions and to name fractions. They will also use their strips to find and name equivalent fractions. The strips will be used again in Lessons 2–5.

Key Content

- Representing fractions using paper folding and symbols.
- Defining numerator and denominator.
- Identifying fractional parts of a whole.
- Comparing fractions using manipulatives.

Key Vocabulary

- denominator
- equivalent fraction
- fraction
- numerator

Math Facts

DPP items B and C and Home Practice Part 1 review and provide practice with the division facts for the nines.

Homework

1. Assign homework *Questions 1–7* in the *Student Guide* any time after Part 1, homework *Questions 8–13* after Part 2, and homework *Questions 14–21* after Part 3.
2. Students take their flash cards home to study the division facts for the nines.
3. Assign Home Practice Part 2 in the *Discovery Assignment Book.*

Assessment

Use the *Observational Assessment Record* to record students' abilities to represent fractions with paper folding.

Curriculum Sequence

Before This Unit

In third grade, students explored fraction concepts in Units 13 and 17. They named fractions, found equivalent fractions, and compared fractions. In Unit 15, students investigated decimals and made connections between decimals and common fractions.

In fourth grade, students investigated decimal fractions in Unit 10.

After This Unit

Students will use fractions in their study of probability in Unit 14. They will learn paper-and-pencil methods for the operations of addition, subtraction, and multi-

plication of fractions in fifth grade. See Grade 5 Units 3, 5, 11, and 12.

Materials List

Supplies and Copies

Student	Teacher
Supplies for Each Student • scissors • 2 envelopes (1 for flash cards and 1 for fraction strips) • crayons, markers, or colored pencils • ruler	**Supplies**
Copies	**Copies/Transparencies** • 1 copy of *Fraction Strips for the Teacher* (*Unit Resource Guide* Pages 42–43) • 1 copy of *Observational Assessment Record* to be used throughout this unit (*Unit Resource Guide* Pages 13–14)

All blackline masters including assessment, transparency, and DPP masters are also on the Teacher Resource CD.

Student Books
Fraction Strips (*Student Guide* Page 326–332)
Triangle Flash Cards: 9s (*Discovery Assignment Book* Page 197)
Making Fraction Strips (*Discovery Assignment Book* Pages 199–201)

Daily Practice and Problems and Home Practice
DPP items A–F (*Unit Resource Guide* Pages 16–19)
Home Practice Parts 1–2 (*Discovery Assignment Book* Page 193)

Note: Classrooms whose pacing differs significantly from the suggested pacing of the units should use the Math Facts Calendar in Section 4 of the *Facts Resource Guide* to ensure students receive the complete math facts program.

Assessment Tools
Observational Assessment Record (*Unit Resource Guide* Pages 13–14)

Daily Practice and Problems

Suggestions for using the DPPs are on page 39.

A. Bit: Telling Time (URG p. 16)

How much time has passed from:

A. 12:10 to 12:30?   B. 1:45 to 2:05?
C. 3:20 to 4:00?   D. 5:25 to 5:55?
E. 11:10 to 12:25?

B. Task: Division Facts: 9s (URG p. 17)

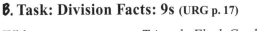

With a partner, use your *Triangle Flash Cards: 9s* to quiz each other on the division facts for the nines. Ask your partner first to cover the numbers in the squares. Use the two uncovered numbers to solve a division fact. Separate the flash cards into three piles: those facts you know and can answer quickly, those you can figure out with a strategy, and those you need to learn.

Then go through the cards again and have your partner cover the numbers in the circles. Use the uncovered numbers to solve a division fact. Separate the cards into three piles again.

Both times through, practice the facts that are in the last two piles and make a list of these facts so you can practice them at home.

Circle all the facts you know and can answer quickly on your *Division Facts I Know* chart.

Repeat this process for your partner.

C. Bit: Division Facts (URG p. 18)

A. 81 ÷ 9 =   B. 9 ÷ 9 =
C. 63 ÷ 9 =   D. 27 ÷ 9 =
E. 36 ÷ 9 =   F. 54 ÷ 9 =
G. 18 ÷ 9 =   H. 72 ÷ 9 =
I. 9 ÷ 1 =   J. 45 ÷ 9 =

D. Task: Multiplication (URG p. 18)

Use paper and pencil or mental math to solve the following problems. Estimate to make sure your answers are reasonable.

1. A. $53 \times 4 =$ B. $459 \times 4 =$
   C. $5532 \times 4 =$ D. $26 \times 45 =$
   E. $22 \times 7 =$ F. $724 \times 3 =$
   G. $3096 \times 5 =$ H. $38 \times 52 =$

2. Explain your strategy for Question 1A.
3. Explain your estimation strategy for Question 1D.

E. Bit: Decimals in Sequence (URG p. 18)

Write the next 3 decimals:

A. 1.0   1.5   2.0   2.5   3.0   __ __ __

B. 6.4   6.8   7.2   7.6   8.0   __ __ __

C. 2.2   3.2   4.2   5.2   6.2   __ __ __

F. Task: Earning an Allowance (URG p. 19)

Irma's aunt pays her 5 cents for each minute she reads a book instead of watching television. She began reading at 4:48 and finished at 5:19. How much money did she make? Tell the strategies you used to get your answer.

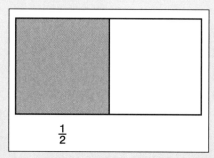

Figure 2: $\frac{1}{2}$ *of a rectangle*

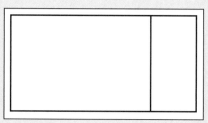

Figure 3: *This rectangle is not divided in half.*

Using the *Fraction Strips for the Teacher* Blackline Masters, cut out, color, and fold one set of fraction strips to use as a class sample.

Students have worked with fraction concepts since first grade. They have used physical models to identify and compare fractions. This, however, is the first concentrated study of common fractions in fourth grade. Before starting this lesson, assess students' prior knowledge about fractions. Draw a rectangle on the board or on an overhead transparency. Tell students that the rectangle is equal to one whole. Divide the rectangle in half and shade one part of the rectangle. Ask students to identify the fraction name for the shaded part of the rectangle. Write the fraction $\frac{1}{2}$ under the shaded part of the rectangle as shown in Figure 2.

Draw a second rectangle and divide it into two obviously unequal pieces as shown in Figure 3. Ask:

- *Does each of these parts also equal $\frac{1}{2}$?* (These pieces do not equal $\frac{1}{2}$ because they are not equal shares.)

If you feel students need other examples of fractions, draw additional rectangles, dividing them to represent various fractions. For example:

- Divide a rectangle into four equal parts. Shade in one part or $\frac{1}{4}$ of the rectangle and ask students to identify how much of the rectangle is shaded. Ask students to identify the fraction of the rectangle that is not shaded ($\frac{3}{4}$).

- Divide a rectangle into three equal parts. Shade in two parts or $\frac{2}{3}$ of the rectangle and ask students to identify how much of the rectangle is shaded. How much of the rectangle is not shaded?

Another way to review fractions is to ask five students, some boys and some girls, to stand in the front of the room. Ask students to identify the fraction of the students who are boys and the fraction who are girls. This activity can be repeated using a different number of students or different attributes each time. For example:

- *What fraction of the students standing have brown hair?*

- *What fraction of the students standing are wearing red today?*

As students call out fractions, write them on the board. Identify the bottom number of each fraction as the **denominator.** Explain that the denominator tells you the number of equal pieces (or parts) that the whole is divided into. Identify the top number of each fraction as the **numerator.** Explain that the numerator tells you how many pieces (or parts) you are interested in.

Part 1 Halves, Fourths, and Eighths

Once you review what a fraction is, begin the paper-folding activity. Students will complete Lesson 1 over three days. They will use their strips during Lesson 2 to add and subtract fractions with like denominators, during Lesson 3 to compare fractions, during Lesson 4 as a chart to play *Frabble,* and during Lesson 5 as a chart to explore equivalent fractions.

Have student work with partners or in small groups so they can discuss strategies. They can also check each other's folds for accuracy.

Give each student an envelope to store the strips. Have students carefully cut out all of the strips on the *Making Fraction Strips* Activity Pages in the *Discovery Assignment Book.* Students will use four of the strips during Part 1. They will identify one strip as a whole and fold the other three into halves, fourths, and eighths. Completed strips should be color-coded. Extra strips can be stored in the envelopes provided.

The first step is to establish that an unfolded strip of paper represents one whole. Tell each student to label an unfolded strip as one whole and set this aside.

Explain to students that they will fold each strip to show different fractions. Have students fold a strip into two pieces that are exactly the same size. Make sure students crease their strips carefully, making

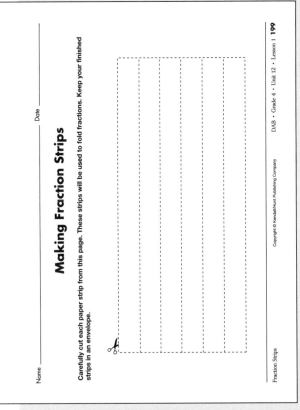

Discovery Assignment Book - page 199

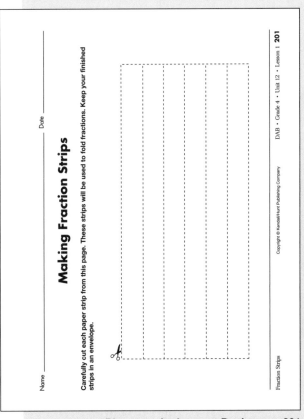

Discovery Assignment Book - page 201

Each student has two extra strips. These can be used if a student loses a strip or makes an error folding. Fraction strips can also be made from construction paper or card stock. Strips should each be 20 cm in length. Each student will need 10 strips of different colors.

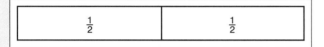

Figure 4: *A paper strip folded into halves*

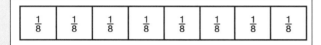

Figure 5: *A fraction strip showing eighths*

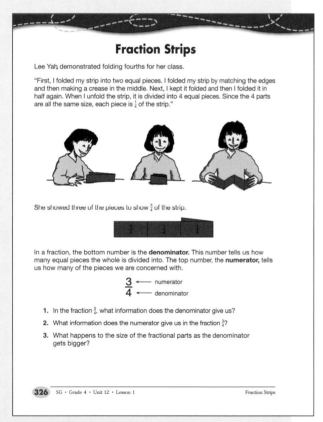

Student Guide - page 326 *(Answers on p. 44)*

clean sharp folds. Once the folding is complete, have students unfold their strips and draw a line with a ruler showing their folds. Ask:

- *What is the fraction name for each part of this strip?* ($\frac{1}{2}$)
- *What is the **denominator** and what does it tell us?* (2, how many parts the whole was divided into)
- *What is the **numerator** and what does it tell us?* (1, how many parts we are concerned with)

Have students color their strips according to the color code decided upon and label each part $\frac{1}{2}$. See Figure 4.

Next, ask students how they can fold a different strip into four equal pieces. Allow students a minute or two to discuss this with members of their groups. Students can first fold their strips in half and then in half again. When they unfold their strips, they will have four equal pieces. After students complete their folds, ask them to unfold their strips and use their rulers to draw a line showing each fold. Ask students what the denominator will be for each fraction on this strip. Students then color their strips and label each section with $\frac{1}{4}$.

Next, students fold a strip into eight equal pieces. Have them discuss a method for doing this within their groups. The most efficient method is first to fold the strip in half, then fold the folded strip in half again, and finally fold this in half. When the strip is unfolded, it will be in eight equal sections. Review the same questions as above for halves. Students should color and label as in Figure 5.

Questions 1–3 on the *Fraction Strips* Activity Pages in the *Student Guide* review what a fraction is, the definition of the denominator, and of the numerator. Use these pages at any time during this lesson to review these concepts.

Show Me. In this activity, students use their fraction strips to represent different fractions. Students will need all their completed strips and the strip representing one whole. To start this activity, name a fraction that can be represented using the fraction strips; for example, $\frac{3}{8}$. To show $\frac{3}{8}$, students should use the strip that is divided into eight equal pieces. They fold $\frac{5}{8}$ of the strip back and leave $\frac{3}{8}$ of the strip showing as in Figure 6.

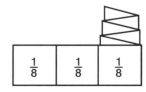

Figure 6: *Folding a strip to show $\frac{3}{8}$*

Continue this activity by asking students to show you fractions that are less than one, for example, $\frac{1}{4}, \frac{5}{8}, \frac{1}{2}, \frac{2}{4}, \frac{3}{4}$.

Once students are comfortable using their strips to show fractions less than one, move on to fractions equivalent to one, such as $\frac{4}{4}$ and $\frac{2}{2}$. Finally, ask students to show mixed numbers—for example, $1\frac{1}{2}$. Point out that to show $1\frac{1}{2}$, students will need to use two of their strips, the strip showing one whole and the strip showing halves.

For a variation of this activity, hold up one of the marked fraction strips you prepared before class. Then, fold it to represent a fraction and ask students to identify the fraction. If students are unable to name the fraction, unfold the strip and ask students to identify the number of parts that the whole strip is divided into (the denominator), then refold the strip to show your fraction and ask how many parts you are showing them (the numerator). Remind students of the definitions of denominator and numerator. Again ask students to name the fraction you are holding.

Assign *Questions 1–7* in the Homework section of the *Student Guide* at this point in the lesson.

Part 2 **Thirds, Sixths, Ninths, and Twelfths**
During this part of the lesson, students will use four more of their strips, folding them into thirds, sixths, ninths, and twelfths. Ask students to take one of their strips and to think about how they can fold it into three equal parts. Students may suggest first folding the strip into a loose "S" and then carefully matching edges before creasing the folds. Students may also suggest folding the paper like a letter. Both techniques are shown in Figure 7.

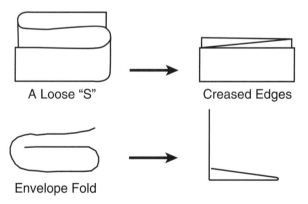

Figure 7: *Folding a strip to show thirds*

Folding strips into thirds is more difficult than the previous folding, so monitor each student's progress carefully. This process may require some trial and

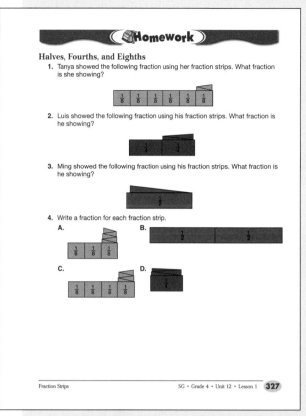

Student Guide - page 327 (Answers on p. 44)

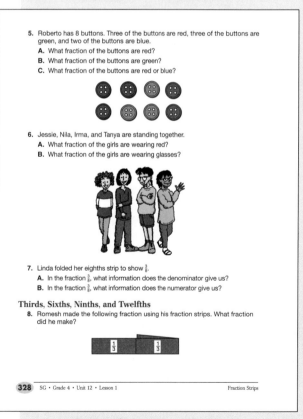

Student Guide - page 328 (Answers on p. 45)

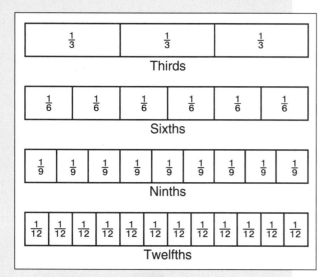

Figure 8: *Thirds, sixths, ninths, and twelfths*

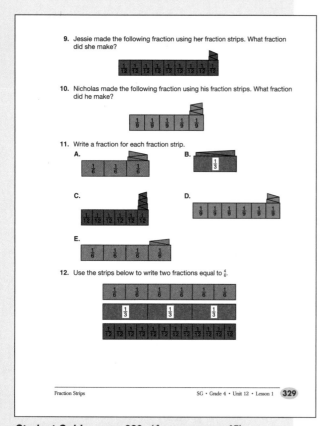

Student Guide - page 329 *(Answers on p. 45)*

error. Students should mark each fold with a line, color their strips, and label each piece $\frac{1}{3}$. Continue this lesson by asking students to discuss methods for folding one strip into six equal pieces or sixths, one strip into nine equal pieces or ninths, and one strip into twelve equal pieces or twelfths.

Students can fold a strip into sixths by first folding it into thirds and then folding the folded strip in half. Students can also start by folding their strips in half and then folding the halves into thirds.

To fold a strip into ninths, students can first fold a strip into thirds and then fold it into thirds again.

A strip can be folded into twelfths by first folding it into thirds, then folding the folded strip in half, and finally folding it in half again, or the strip can first be folded in half, then thirds, and finally in half again. As students fold each strip, they should mark their folds with a line, color, and label each strip with the correct fraction name as shown in Figure 8.

Students have now completed strips to show one whole, halves, thirds, fourths, sixths, eighths, ninths, and twelfths. Ask students to lay all eight strips out on their desks. You can now extend Show Me, described in Part 1 of this lesson, to include all eight strips.

Equivalent Fractions. This part of the activity is initially teacher-led. However, once students are comfortable with this procedure, have them work with a partner to find equivalent fractions. Ask:

• *Fold your halves strips to show $\frac{1}{2}$. Find and fold all the other strips that can be folded to show the same quantity.*

Remind students that strips can only be folded on existing fraction lines. Figure 9 illustrates those fraction strips that can be folded to show fractions equal to $\frac{1}{2}$.

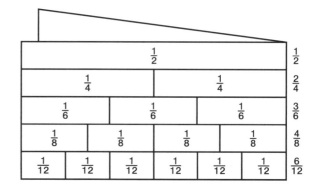

Figure 9: *Folding fractions equivalent to $\frac{1}{2}$*

List all the equivalencies on the board. The list should include $\frac{1}{2}$, $\frac{2}{4}$, $\frac{3}{6}$, $\frac{4}{8}$, and $\frac{6}{12}$. Explain that these are

called **equivalent fractions** because they each show the same part of the whole. Ask:

- *Which strips cannot be folded on existing fraction lines to show an equivalent fraction for $\frac{1}{2}$?* (Students will see that they cannot use the strip divided into thirds and the strip divided into ninths to show a fraction equivalent to $\frac{1}{2}$.)

- *Look at the denominators of the strips that can show a fraction equivalent to $\frac{1}{2}$ and then at the strips that cannot show an equivalent fraction. What can you say about the denominators that can show fractions equivalent to $\frac{1}{2}$?*

Guide students to see that when the denominator is a multiple of two, a fraction equivalent to $\frac{1}{2}$ can be found, but when the denominator is not a multiple of two there is not an equivalent fraction with that denominator. Continue this activity in a similar fashion with $\frac{1}{3}$ and $\frac{1}{4}$.

- *What are all the fractions that are equivalent to $\frac{1}{3}$?* ($\frac{2}{6}, \frac{3}{9}, \frac{4}{12}$)

- *What do you notice about these denominators?* (They are all multiples of 3.)

Suggest other fractions for the students to find equivalent fractions, e.g., $\frac{1}{4}, \frac{3}{4}, \frac{2}{3}, \frac{5}{6}$, etc.

Assign *Questions 8–13* in the Homework section of the *Student Guide* at this time.

Part 3 **Fifths and Tenths**

Students will use the two strips left from Parts 1 and 2 of this lesson, folding one into five equal pieces or fifths and one strip into ten equal pieces or tenths. Ask students for a strategy to fold a strip into five equal pieces. Students will probably realize that this is a very difficult task without something to guide them. Students may suggest using their rulers to find out how long each strip is. See Figure 10. They can then

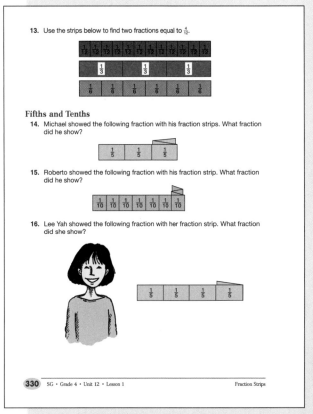

Student Guide - page 330 (Answers on p. 46)

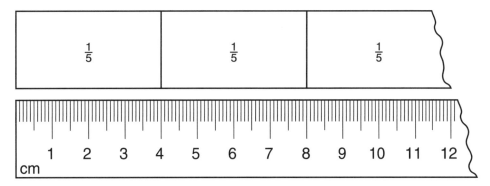

Figure 10: *Measuring 5 equal pieces*

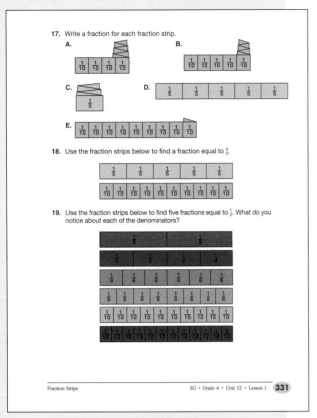

Student Guide - page 331 (Answers on p. 46)

divide to find out how long each piece should be. The strips are each 20 cm long. This means that when dividing into fifths, each piece should be four cm long and when dividing into tenths, each piece should be two cm long. Students can use their rulers to mark each fold before making the creases. This method is shown in Figure 10. Make sure students draw lines to show their folds, color their strips, and label each $\frac{1}{5}$.

To fold a strip into ten equal pieces, students can first fold their strips into fifths and then fold these folded strips in half. Students can also use their rulers to find where each fold should be. Students should mark folds, color, and label as before.

Students now have a complete set of fraction strips. This set should include one whole strip and strips folded into 2, 3, 4, 5, 6, 8, 9, 10, and 12 equal pieces. Extend the Show Me activity described in Part 1 of this lesson and Equivalent Fractions described in Part 2 using the complete set of fraction strips. Store the fraction strips in envelopes for use during Lessons 2–3.

Assign *Questions 14–21* in the Homework section of the *Student Guide* at this time.

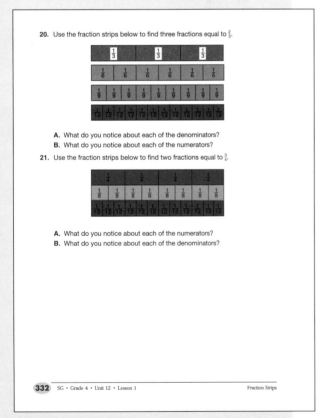

Student Guide - page 332 (Answers on p. 47)

Math Facts

- Use DPP items B and C to begin the review and practice of the division facts for the nines.
- Part 1 of the Home Practice reminds students to take home their flash cards to practice the facts.

Homework and Practice

- Assign the homework questions in the *Student Guide* as appropriate. **Questions 1–7** can be assigned after Part 1, **Questions 8–13** after Part 2, and **Questions 14–21** after Part 3.
- DPP items A and F provide practice with elapsed time. Use Task D for practice with multidigit multiplication. DPP Bit E requires students to extend a pattern using decimals.
- Assign Part 2 of the Home Practice.

Answers for Part 2 of the Home Practice are in the Answer Key at the end of this lesson and at the end of this unit.

Assessment

Use the *Observational Assessment Record* to document students' abilities to represent fractions using paper folding.

Name _____ Date _____

Unit 12 Home Practice

PART 1 *Triangle Flash Cards: 9s*
Study for the quiz on the division facts for the nines. Take home your *Triangle Flash Cards: 9s* and your list of facts you need to study.

Ask a family member to choose one flash card at a time. He or she should cover one of the smaller numbers. (One of the smaller numbers is circled. The other has a square around it.) Solve a division fact using the two uncovered numbers. Ask your family member to sometimes cover the circled numbers and sometimes cover the number in the square.

Your teacher will tell you when the quiz on the nines will be.

PART 2 **Multiplication**

1. Solve the following problems in your head. Remember to follow the proper order of operations.

   A. $87 \times 0 =$ _____   B. $211 \times 1 =$ _____
   C. $0 \times 1800 =$ _____   D. $1 \times 7898 =$ _____
   E. $8 \times 0 + 8 =$ _____   F. $7 + 1 \times 10 =$ _____
   G. $16 \times 1 - 7 =$ _____   H. $6 \times 1 - 2 \times 0 =$ _____
   I. $20 - 0 \times 7 =$ _____   J. $20 \times 7 - 0 =$ _____

2. Explain why all the multiples of 6 are even numbers. First, write all the multiples of 6 in order from 6 to 60.

EXPLORING FRACTIONS   DAB • Grade 4 • Unit 12 **193**

Discovery Assignment Book - page 193 (Answers on p. 47)

Name _____ Date _____

Triangle Flash Cards: 9s

- Work with a partner. Each partner cuts out the flash cards below.
- To quiz you on a division fact, your partner covers the number in the square. Solve a division fact with the two uncovered numbers.
- Divide the cards into three piles: those facts you know and can answer quickly, those you can figure out with a strategy, and those you need to learn.
- Practice the last two piles again. Then make a list of the facts you need to practice at home.
- Go through the cards again. This time your partner covers the numbers in the circles.
- Sort the cards into the three piles. Make a list of the facts you need to practice at home.
- Repeat the directions for your partner.

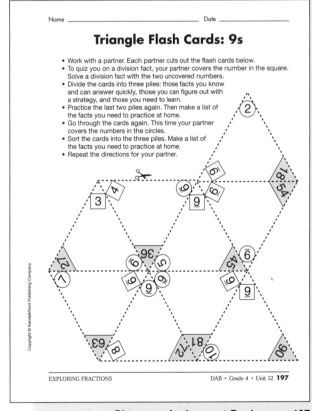

EXPLORING FRACTIONS   DAB • Grade 4 • Unit 12 **197**

Discovery Assignment Book - page 197

At a Glance

Math Facts and Daily Practice and Problems

DPP items B and C and Home Practice Part 1 review and practice the division facts for the nines. DPP Items A and F provide practice with time. DPP Task D practices multiplication and DPP Bit E asks students to extend a decimal pattern.

Before the Activity

1. Use the *Fraction Strips for the Teacher* Blackline Masters to make one set of fraction strips for demonstration.
2. Review fractions using fractions on the board. Define numerator and denominator.
3. Model fractions of a set with a group of students.

Part 1. Halves, Fourths, and Eighths

1. Students cut out 20-cm paper strips on the *Making Fraction Strips* Activity Pages in the *Discovery Assignment Book.*
2. Students label one strip as a whole and set this aside.
3. Each student folds one strip into two equal pieces, marks the fold, labels each piece $\frac{1}{2}$, and colors the strip.
4. Students follow the same procedure to make strips for fourths and eighths.
5. Introduce the Show Me activity, in which you name a fraction and the students show the same fraction using the strips.
6. Use the first *Fraction Strips* Activity Page in the *Student Guide* to review the definition of numerator and denominator.

Part 2. Thirds, Sixths, Ninths, and Twelfths

1. Students follow the above procedure to make strips for thirds, sixths, ninths, and twelfths. Extend Show Me to include all eight of their strips.
2. Introduce Equivalent Fractions, in which you name a fraction and students find all the equivalent fractions they can make using their strips.

Part 3. Fifths and Tenths

1. Students use their rulers to divide one strip into fifths and one strip into tenths.
2. Students color each strip and label each piece with the correct fraction name.
3. Extend Show Me and Equivalent Fractions to include all ten strips.
4. Save all strips in envelopes for use during Lessons 2–5.

Homework

1. Assign homework *Questions 1–7* in the *Student Guide* any time after Part 1, homework *Questions 8–13* after Part 2, and homework *Questions 14–21* after Part 3.
2. Students take their flash cards home to study the division facts for the nines.
3. Assign Home Practice Part 2 in the *Discovery Assignment Book.*

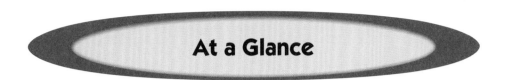

At a Glance

Name

Date

Fraction Strips for the Teacher

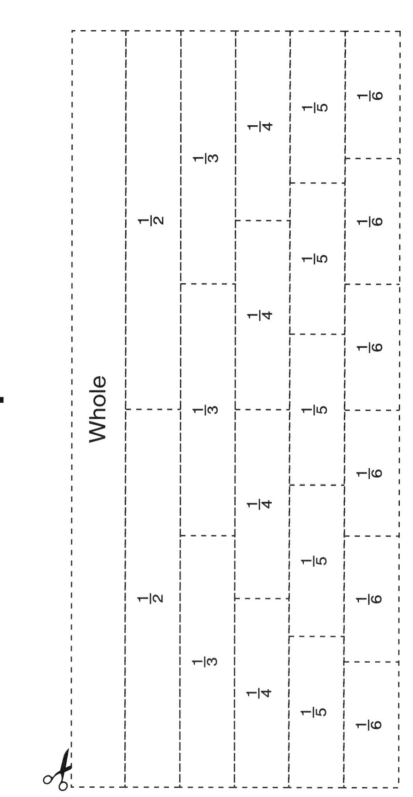

Fraction Strips for the Teacher

$\frac{1}{8}$	$\frac{1}{8}$	$\frac{1}{8}$	$\frac{1}{8}$	$\frac{1}{8}$	$\frac{1}{8}$	$\frac{1}{8}$	$\frac{1}{8}$
$\frac{1}{9}$	$\frac{1}{9}$	$\frac{1}{9}$	$\frac{1}{9}$	$\frac{1}{9}$	$\frac{1}{9}$	$\frac{1}{9}$	$\frac{1}{9}$	$\frac{1}{9}$
$\frac{1}{10}$	$\frac{1}{10}$	$\frac{1}{10}$	$\frac{1}{10}$	$\frac{1}{10}$	$\frac{1}{10}$	$\frac{1}{10}$	$\frac{1}{10}$	$\frac{1}{10}$	$\frac{1}{10}$
$\frac{1}{12}$	$\frac{1}{12}$	$\frac{1}{12}$	$\frac{1}{12}$	$\frac{1}{12}$	$\frac{1}{12}$	$\frac{1}{12}$	$\frac{1}{12}$	$\frac{1}{12}$	$\frac{1}{12}$	$\frac{1}{12}$	$\frac{1}{12}$

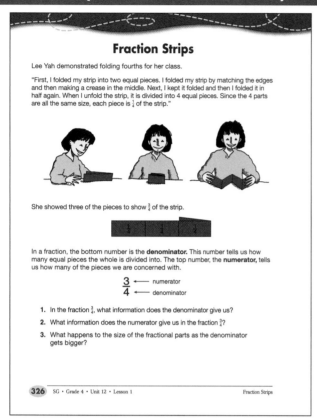

Student Guide - page 326

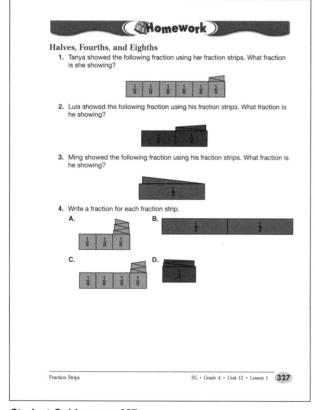

Student Guide - page 327

Student Guide (p. 326)

Fraction Strips

1. The denominator tells the number of equal parts that the whole is divided into.

2. The numerator tells how many parts you are interested in.

3. The fraction gets smaller

Student Guide (p. 327)

Homework

1. $\frac{6}{8}$

2. $\frac{2}{4}$

3. $\frac{1}{2}$

4. A. $\frac{3}{8}$

   B. $\frac{2}{2}$ or 1

   C. $\frac{4}{8}$

   D. $\frac{1}{4}$

Student Guide (p. 328)

5. **A.** $\frac{3}{8}$

   B. $\frac{3}{8}$

   C. $\frac{5}{8}$

6. **A.** $\frac{3}{4}$

   B. $\frac{2}{4}$ or $\frac{1}{2}$

7. **A.** The denominator tells us that the fraction strip is divided into 8 equal pieces.

   B. The numerator tells us she is showing 3 of the 8 pieces.

8. $\frac{2}{3}$

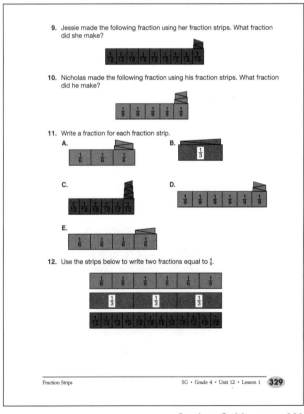

Student Guide - page 328

Student Guide (p. 329)

9. $\frac{9}{12}$

10. $\frac{5}{9}$

11. **A.** $\frac{3}{6}$

   B. $\frac{1}{3}$

   C. $\frac{6}{12}$

   D. $\frac{6}{9}$

   E. $\frac{4}{6}$

12. $\frac{2}{3}, \frac{8}{12}$

Student Guide - page 329

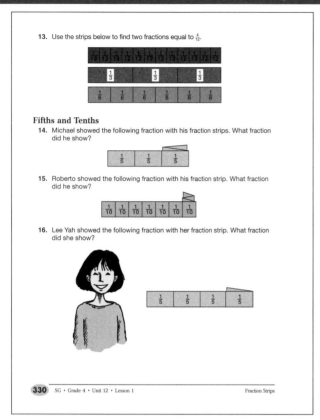

Student Guide - page 330

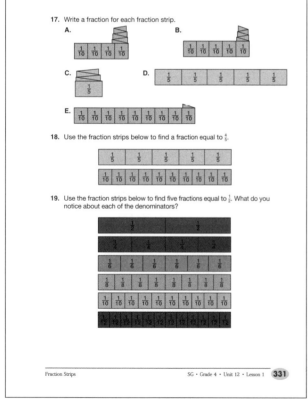

Student Guide - page 331

Student Guide (p. 330)

13. $\frac{1}{3}, \frac{2}{6}$

14. $\frac{3}{5}$

15. $\frac{7}{10}$

16. $\frac{4}{5}$

Student Guide (p. 331)

17. A. $\frac{4}{10}$

    B. $\frac{5}{10}$ or $\frac{1}{2}$

    C. $\frac{1}{5}$

    D. $\frac{5}{5}$ or 1

    E. $\frac{9}{10}$

18. $\frac{8}{10}$

19. $\frac{2}{4}, \frac{3}{6}, \frac{4}{8}, \frac{5}{10}, \frac{6}{12}$

Each denominator is even and, therefore, a multiple of 2.

Student Guide (p. 332)

20. $\frac{4}{6}, \frac{6}{9}, \frac{8}{12}$

A. Each denominator is a multiple of 3.

B. Each numerator is even and, therefore, a multiple of 2.

21. $\frac{6}{8}, \frac{9}{12}$

A. Both the numerators are multiples of 3.

B. Both the denominators are multiples of 4.

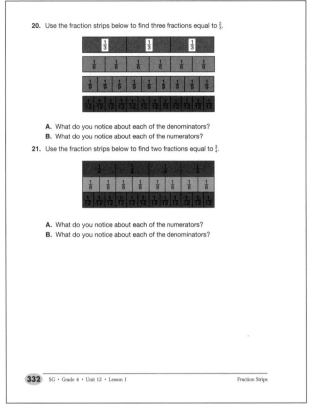

Student Guide - page 332

Discovery Assignment Book (p. 193)

Home Practice*

Part 2. Multiplication

1. **A.** 0   **B.** 211

     C. 0   **D.** 7898

     E. 8   **F.** 17

     G. 9   **H.** 6

     I. 20   **J.** 140

2. 6, 12, 18, 24, 30, 36, 42, 48, 54, 60

An even number has 2 as a factor. Since 2 is a factor of 6, 2 is a factor of all the multiples of 6. So, all multiples of 6 are even numbers.

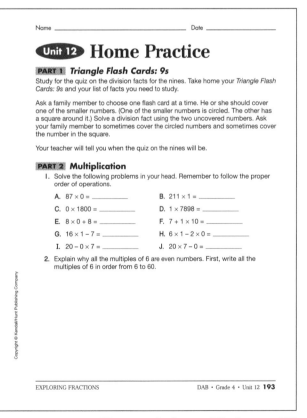

Discovery Assignment Book - page 193

*Answers for all the Home Practice in the *Discovery Assignment Book* are at the end of the unit.

Lesson 2

Adding and Subtracting with Fraction Strips

Lesson Overview

Students use their fraction strips from Lesson 1 to add and subtract fractions with like denominators.

Key Content

- Adding and subtracting fractions with like denominators.

Math Facts

DPP Bit G provides practice with division facts and Task H provides practice with prime factorization.

Homework

Assign homework *Questions 1–7* in the *Student Guide.* Students will need their fraction strips.

Assessment

Use the *Observational Assessment Record* to note students' progress adding and subtracting fractions with like denominators using manipulatives.

Materials List

Supplies and Copies

Student	Teacher
Supplies for Each Student Pair • 1 set of fraction strips from Lesson 1	**Supplies**
Copies	**Copies/Transparencies** • 1 set of cut strips, folded, colored, and labeled copied from *Fraction Strips for the Teacher* (*Unit Resource Guide* Pages 42–43)

All blackline masters including assessment, transparency, and DPP masters are also on the Teacher Resource CD.

Student Books
Adding and Subtracting with Fraction Strips (*Student Guide* Pages 333–335)

Daily Practice and Problems and Home Practice
DPP items G–H (*Unit Resource Guide* Page 19)

Note: Classrooms whose pacing differs significantly from the suggested pacing of the units should use the Math Facts Calendar in Section 4 of the *Facts Resource Guide* to ensure students receive the complete math facts program.

Assessment Tools
Observational Assessment Record (*Unit Resource Guide* Pages 13–14)

Daily Practice and Problems

Suggestions for using the DPPs are on page 51.

G. Bit: More Division Facts (URG p. 19)

Find the number *n* that makes the sentence true.

A. $72 \div 8 = n$ B. $n \div 9 = 6$
C. $n \div 9 = 5$ D. $36 \div 4 = n$
E. $27 \div n = 9$ F. $n \div 9 = 9$
G. $n \div 9 = 2$ H. $63 \div n = 9$

H. Task: Prime Factors (URG p. 19)

1. Which of the following are prime numbers?

   53   54   57   67   96   103

2. For the composite numbers, use factor trees to factor them into a product of primes. You may use a calculator.

Student Guide - page 333

Adding and Subtracting with Fraction Strips

Mrs. Dewey asked her class to use their fraction strips to add $\frac{1}{4}$ and $\frac{2}{4}$. Keenya explained her solution to the class:

"First, I folded my strip that shows fourths so that 1 piece or $\frac{1}{4}$ of the strip was showing. Then, I added $\frac{2}{4}$ of the strip by unfolding 2 more pieces. I ended up with $\frac{3}{4}$ of my strip showing. So, $\frac{1}{4} + \frac{2}{4} = \frac{3}{4}$."

Next, Mrs. Dewey asked the class to use their fraction strips to subtract $\frac{3}{8}$ from $\frac{7}{8}$.

Jacob explained his solution to the class:

"I started with my strip that is divided into eighths. I folded it so that $\frac{7}{8}$ of the strip was showing. Then I folded back $\frac{3}{8}$ of the strip or 3 more pieces since I was subtracting. This left me with $\frac{4}{8}$ of the strip showing, so $\frac{7}{8} - \frac{3}{8} = \frac{4}{8}$."

Adding and Subtracting with Fraction Strips   SG • Grade 4 • Unit 12 • Lesson 2   **333**

Student Guide - page 333

Student Guide - page 334 (Answers on p. 53)

Work with a partner to solve the following problems. You will need to use two sets of fraction strips. Write a number sentence for each problem.

1. Maya has $\frac{5}{8}$ of a yard of fabric. She needs $\frac{3}{8}$ of a yard of fabric for a craft project. How much fabric will she have left over after she completes her project?

2. Frank is baking a cake. The recipe calls for $\frac{1}{4}$ cup of oil and $\frac{3}{4}$ cup of water. How much liquid will Frank add to the cake mix?

3. Jessie used $\frac{5}{12}$ of a board for a sign. What fraction of the board is left for another project?

4. There was $\frac{5}{6}$ of a pie on the counter when Luis got home from school.
   A. Luis ate $\frac{2}{6}$ of the pie. How much of the pie is left?
   B. Luis's sister ate another $\frac{1}{6}$ of the pie. Now how much of the pie is left?
   C. Use your fraction strips to find another fraction that is equal to your answer to Question 4B.

5. Ming rode his bike $\frac{8}{10}$ mile to Frank's house. He then rode $\frac{8}{10}$ mile back home. How far did Ming ride altogether?

6. Irma must finish her homework and practice piano before she can go outside to play. It takes her $\frac{3}{4}$ hour to do her homework, and she practices piano for $\frac{2}{4}$ hour. How long does she have to wait before going outside to play?

7. Use your fraction strips to complete the following number sentences.
   A. $\frac{3}{8} + \frac{2}{8} =$ B. $\frac{7}{10} + \frac{5}{10} =$ C. $\frac{3}{6} + \frac{3}{6} =$
   D. $\frac{11}{12} - \frac{4}{12} =$ E. $\frac{3}{5} - \frac{1}{5} =$ F. $\frac{7}{8} - \frac{3}{8} =$

334   SG • Grade 4 • Unit 12 • Lesson 2   Adding and Subtracting with Fraction Strips

Student Guide - page 334 (Answers on p. 53)

Teaching the Activity

Introduce this lesson by reading the short vignette on the *Adding and Subtracting with Fraction Strips* Activity Pages in the *Student Guide*. Then have students use their fraction strips to complete *Questions 1–7*. Students should work with a partner as two sets of fraction strips are needed for some of the questions. Students complete the questions and then share their solutions in class. As you discuss the answers to these questions, draw students' attention to the numerators and the denominators. Help students to see that when you add fractions with like denominators, you add the numerators but the denominator does not change. This is because the size of the fractional part does not change, only the number of pieces you are concerned with.

To solve *Question 1,* students use their eighths strips. They should begin with $\frac{5}{8}$ of the strip showing and then subtract $\frac{3}{8}$ of the strip. They show subtraction by folding back $\frac{3}{8}$ of the strip. Students end with $\frac{2}{8}$ of their strips showing. Their number sentences should read: $\frac{5}{8} - \frac{3}{8} = \frac{2}{8}$.

Both *Questions 2* and *3* reinforce the concept that when the numerator and the denominator are the same number, the fraction indicates one whole. In *Question 2,* students use their fourths strips to add $\frac{1}{4}$ and $\frac{3}{4}$. The number sentence should read: $\frac{1}{4} + \frac{3}{4} = \frac{4}{4}$ or $\frac{1}{4} + \frac{3}{4} = 1$ whole.

To solve *Question 3,* students begin with their twelfths strips. Students should begin with the whole strip and then fold back $\frac{5}{12}$ of the strip to show subtraction. They end up with $\frac{7}{12}$ of the strip. The number sentence is $\frac{12}{12} - \frac{5}{12} = \frac{7}{12}$ or $1 - \frac{5}{12} = \frac{7}{12}$.

Students use their sixths strips to solve *Question 4.* For the first part of this question, begin with $\frac{5}{6}$ of the strip showing. Fold back $\frac{2}{6}$ of the strip. Students are left with $\frac{3}{6}$ of the strip. The number sentence should read: $\frac{5}{6} - \frac{2}{6} = \frac{3}{6}$. For the second part of the question, students start with $\frac{3}{6}$ of their strip. They then fold back $\frac{1}{6}$ of the strip. They are left with $\frac{2}{6}$ of the strip showing. The number sentence is $\frac{3}{6} - \frac{1}{6} = \frac{2}{6}$. *Question 4C* asks students to use their fraction strips to find an equivalent fraction to $\frac{2}{6}$. They need to compare their sixths strip to other fraction strips to find fractions ($\frac{1}{3}$, $\frac{3}{9}$, $\frac{4}{12}$) that are equivalent to $\frac{2}{6}$.

Students need to work with a partner to solve **Questions 5–7**. In **Question 5**, each student will use his or her tenths strip. After adding $\frac{8}{10}$ and $\frac{8}{10}$, students should find that Ming's total trip was $\frac{16}{10}$ miles. Some students may recognize this as $1\frac{6}{10}$ miles; however, not all students will make this connection. Changing improper fractions to mixed numbers will be studied in fifth grade. It is not necessary that students do this at this time. The possible number sentences for **Question 5** are $\frac{8}{10} + \frac{8}{10} = \frac{16}{10}$ or $\frac{8}{10} + \frac{8}{10} = 1\frac{6}{10}$.

To complete **Question 6**, each student pair will use both of their fourths strips. After adding $\frac{3}{4}$ and $\frac{2}{4}$, students should find that Irma must wait $\frac{5}{4}$ hours before going outside. Students may recognize this as $1\frac{1}{4}$ hours. The possible number sentences for **Question 6** are: $\frac{3}{4} + \frac{2}{4} = \frac{5}{4}$ or $\frac{3}{4} + \frac{2}{4} = 1\frac{1}{4}$. Either sentence is acceptable.

Math Facts

DPP Bit G provides review of division facts. Task H uses multiplication facts to review prime numbers, composite numbers, and prime factorization.

Homework and Practice

Assign homework **Questions 1–7** on the *Adding and Subtracting with Fraction Strips* Activity Pages. Students need to take home their fraction strips to solve these problems.

Assessment

- Homework **Questions 1–7** on the *Adding and Subtracting with Fraction Strips* Activity Pages can be used to assess students' abilities to add and subtract fractions with like denominators using manipulatives.

- Use the *Observational Assessment Record* to note students' progress with addition and subtraction of fractions with like denominators.

Journal Prompt

Michael completed the following problem: $\frac{3}{8} + \frac{2}{8} = \frac{5}{16}$. Is his answer correct? Why or why not?

Homework

Use your fraction strips to complete the following problems. Write a number sentence for each problem.

1. Grace needed $\frac{5}{8}$ of a yard of ribbon to decorate the outside edge of a picture frame. She needed another $\frac{3}{8}$ of a yard of ribbon to decorate the inside edge of her frame. How much ribbon did she need to finish the frame?

2. **A.** On Monday, John ate $\frac{1}{6}$ of a box of cookies. On Tuesday, he ate another $\frac{2}{6}$ of the cookies. What fraction of the cookies did he eat altogether?
   B. What fraction of the cookies is left?

3. **A.** Jerome lives $\frac{7}{10}$ of a mile from school. If he has already walked $\frac{3}{10}$ of a mile, how much farther does he have to go before he gets to school?
   B. Use your fraction strips to find another fraction that is equal to your answer.

4. Tanya and Nila used their fraction strips to add fractions. Look at their work. Write a number sentence to show what they did.

Tanya's Strip   +   Nila's Strip

5. Use your fraction strips to complete the following number sentences.
   A. $\frac{1}{12} + \frac{4}{12} =$ **B.** $\frac{7}{10} - \frac{5}{10} =$ **C.** $\frac{5}{8} + \frac{3}{8} =$

6. Maya and Jerome used their fraction strips to show the following addition problem. Write a number sentence for their work.

Maya's Strip   +   Jerome's Strip

7. Michael and his brother shared a pizza.
   A. Michael ate $\frac{2}{8}$ of a whole pizza. How much pizza was left?
   B. His brother ate another $\frac{3}{8}$ of the whole pizza. How much pizza was left?
   C. How much pizza did Michael and his brother eat altogether?

Adding and Subtracting with Fraction Strips   SG • Grade 4 • Unit 12 • Lesson 2   **335**

Student Guide - page 335 (Answers on p. 53)

Math Facts and Daily Practice and Problems

DPP Bit G provides practice with division facts and Task H provides practice with prime factorization.

Teaching the Activity

1. Read the vignette on the *Adding and Subtracting with Fraction Strips* Activity Pages in the *Student Guide.*
2. Review Keenya's and Jacob's solutions to the problems presented.
3. Students in pairs use their fraction strips to complete *Questions 1–7.* Discuss students' strategies.

Homework

Assign homework *Questions 1–7* in the *Student Guide.* Students will need their fraction strips.

Assessment

Use the *Observational Assessment Record* to note students' progress adding and subtracting fractions with like denominators using manipulatives.

Answer Key is on page 53.

Notes:

Student Guide (p. 334)

1. $\frac{2}{8}$ yd*

2. $\frac{4}{4}$ or 1 cup*

3. $\frac{7}{12}$*

4. **A.** $\frac{3}{6}$ pie*

   B. $\frac{2}{6}$ pie

   C. $\frac{1}{3}, \frac{3}{9}, \frac{4}{12}$

5. $\frac{16}{10}$ or $1\frac{6}{10}$ miles (Accept either the improper fraction or mixed number.)*

6. $\frac{5}{4}$ hours or $1\frac{1}{4}$ hours*

7. **A.** $\frac{5}{8}$

   B. $\frac{12}{10}$ or $1\frac{2}{10}$

   C. $\frac{6}{6}$ or 1

   D. $\frac{7}{12}$

   E. $\frac{2}{5}$

   F. $\frac{4}{8}$

Explore

Work with a partner to solve the following problems. You will need to use two sets of fraction strips. Write a number sentence for each problem.

1. Maya has $\frac{6}{8}$ of a yard of fabric. She needs $\frac{3}{8}$ of a yard of fabric for a craft project. How much fabric will she have left over after she completes her project?

2. Frank is baking a cake. The recipe calls for $\frac{1}{4}$ cup of oil and $\frac{3}{4}$ cup of water. How much liquid will Frank add to the cake mix?

3. Jessie used $\frac{5}{12}$ of a board for a sign. What fraction of the board is left for another project?

4. There was $\frac{6}{8}$ of a pie on the counter when Luis got home from school.
   A. Luis ate $\frac{2}{8}$ of the pie. How much of the pie is left?
   B. Luis's sister ate another $\frac{1}{8}$ of the pie. Now how much of the pie is left?
   C. Use your fraction strips to find another fraction that is equal to your answer to Question 4B.

5. Ming rode his bike $\frac{8}{10}$ mile to Frank's house. He then rode $\frac{8}{10}$ mile back home. How far did Ming ride altogether?

6. Irma must finish her homework and practice piano before she can go outside to play. It takes her $\frac{3}{4}$ hour to do her homework, and she practices piano for $\frac{2}{4}$ hour. How long does she have to wait before going outside to play?

7. Use your fraction strips to complete the following number sentences.
   A. $\frac{3}{8} + \frac{2}{8} =$
   B. $\frac{7}{10} + \frac{5}{10} =$
   C. $\frac{3}{6} + \frac{3}{6} =$
   D. $\frac{11}{12} - \frac{4}{12} =$
   E. $\frac{3}{5} - \frac{1}{5} =$
   F. $\frac{7}{8} - \frac{3}{8} =$

334 SG • Grade 4 • Unit 12 • Lesson 2   Adding and Subtracting with Fraction Strips

Student Guide - page 334

Student Guide (p. 335)

1. $\frac{8}{8}$ or 1 yard

2. **A.** $\frac{3}{5}$ of a box

   B. $\frac{2}{5}$ of a box

3. **A.** $\frac{4}{10}$ of a mile

   B. $\frac{2}{5}$

4. $\frac{9}{12} + \frac{7}{12} = \frac{16}{12}$ or $1\frac{4}{12}$ (Accept either the improper fraction or mixed number.)

5. **A.** $\frac{5}{12}$

   B. $\frac{2}{10}$

   C. $\frac{8}{8}$ or 1

6. $\frac{6}{9} + \frac{7}{9} = \frac{13}{9}$ or $1\frac{4}{9}$

7. **A.** $\frac{6}{8}$ pizza

   B. $\frac{3}{8}$ pizza

   C. $\frac{5}{8}$ pizza

Homework

Use your fraction strips to complete the following problems. Write a number sentence for each problem.

1. Grace needed $\frac{6}{8}$ of a yard of ribbon to decorate the outside edge of a picture frame. She needed another $\frac{2}{8}$ of a yard of ribbon to decorate the inside edge of her frame. How much ribbon did she need to finish the frame?

2. **A.** On Monday, John ate $\frac{1}{8}$ of a box of cookies. On Tuesday, he ate another $\frac{2}{8}$ of the cookies. What fraction of the cookies did he eat altogether?
   B. What fraction of the cookies is left?

3. **A.** Jerome lives $\frac{7}{10}$ of a mile from school. If he has already walked $\frac{3}{10}$ of a mile, how much farther does he have to go before he gets to school?
   B. Use your fraction strips to find another fraction that is equal to your answer.

4. Tanya and Nila used their fraction strips to add fractions. Look at their work. Write a number sentence to show what they did.

 +

Tanya's Strip   Nila's Strip

5. Use your fraction strips to complete the following number sentences.
   A. $\frac{1}{12} + \frac{4}{12} =$
   B. $\frac{7}{10} - \frac{5}{10} =$
   C. $\frac{5}{8} + \frac{3}{8} =$

6. Maya and Jerome used their fraction strips to show the following addition problem. Write a number sentence for their work.

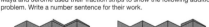 +

Maya's Strip   Jerome's Strip

7. Michael and his brother shared a pizza.
   A. Michael ate $\frac{6}{8}$ of a whole pizza. How much pizza was left?
   B. His brother ate another $\frac{3}{8}$ of the whole pizza. How much pizza was left?
   C. How much pizza did Michael and his brother eat altogether?

Adding and Subtracting with Fraction Strips   SG • Grade 4 • Unit 12 • Lesson 2 335

Student Guide - page 335

*Answers and/or discussion are included in the Lesson Guide.

Comparing Fractions

Lesson Overview

Estimated Class Sessions

1

Students organize their fraction strips in a chart and then use the chart to compare and order fractions according to size.

Key Content

- Comparing fractions using manipulatives.

Key Vocabulary

- benchmark

Homework

Assign homework *Questions 1–8* in the *Student Guide.*

Assessment

Use the *Observational Assessment Record* to note students' abilities to order fractions.

Materials List

Supplies and Copies

Student	Teacher
Supplies for Each Student • glue • sheet of blank paper • 1 set of fraction strips from Lesson 1	**Supplies**
Copies	**Copies/Transparencies** • 1 copy of *Fraction Strips for the Teacher* (*Unit Resource Guide* Pages 42–43) • 1 transparency of *Fraction Chart* (*Unit Resource Guide* Page 61)

All blackline masters including assessment, transparency, and DPP masters are also on the Teacher Resource CD.

Student Books
Comparing Fractions (*Student Guide* Pages 336–338)

Daily Practice and Problems and Home Practice
DPP items I–J (*Unit Resource Guide* Page 20)

Note: Classrooms whose pacing differs significantly from the suggested pacing of the units should use the Math Facts Calendar in Section 4 of the *Facts Resource Guide* to ensure students receive the complete math facts program.

Assessment Tools
Observational Assessment Record (*Unit Resource Guide* Pages 13–14)

I. Bit: Decimals from Pictures (URG p. 20)

Write a decimal for the shaded part of each picture.
The flat is one whole.

1.

2.

3.

4.

J. Task: More Multiplication
   (URG p. 20)

1. Solve the following using a paper-and-pencil
   method.
   A. $239 \times 7 =$ B. $3729 \times 3 =$

   C. $2390 \times 2 =$ D. $79 \times 23 =$

2. Find at least two ways to round each of
   the answers to Questions 1A through 1D.

Using the *Fraction Strips for the Teacher* Blackline Master, cut out, color, and mount one set of fraction strips on a chart as shown in Figure 11. Display this chart in the classroom for use during this lesson.

Teaching the Activity

Pose the following question:

- *Jerome has $\frac{2}{3}$ yard of ribbon and Shannon has $\frac{1}{2}$ yard of ribbon. Who has more ribbon?*

Have students share the strategies they used. Suggest using fraction strips to help answer this question.

Tell students they are going to create a visual tool to make it easy to compare the sizes of different fractions. Each student will need a complete set of fraction strips and a blank sheet of paper for mounting them. To make the chart, students should first experiment with organizing the strips so the charts will be useful for comparing fractions. Ask two or three students:

- *How did you decide to order your fraction strips?*
- *How will the order help you compare fractions?*

For example, students may decide to organize their charts from top to bottom in descending order from the largest-sized piece to the smallest-sized piece. An example of this is shown in Figure 11. Other students may choose to organize their charts by placing the strips in groups of related fractions as shown in Figure 12.

Students will then glue their strips to blank sheets of paper in the order they choose. The only guidelines all students must follow are:

- Be prepared to explain their ordering of the strips. They must be able to show how they will use the chart.
- Place the strips so the long edges line up one against the other.
- Glue strips down so they are touching each other. This makes it easier to compare fractions.
- Line up the left and right edges of all of the strips.

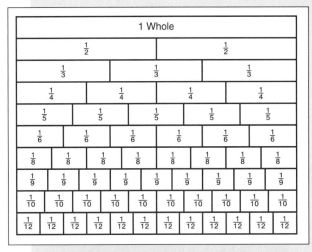

Figure 11: *A fraction chart*

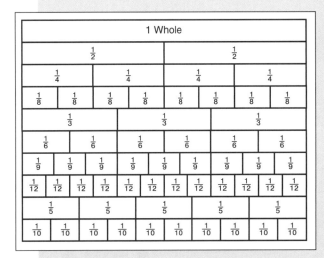

Figure 12: *Another way to organize a fraction chart*

TIMS Tip

The ten fraction strips will fit on an $8\frac{1}{2} \times 11$ inch sheet of paper, if they are placed horizontally as shown in Figures 11 and 12. To help students line up their strips so they are straight, suggest they align their first strip along the top edge of their papers. They can also match either the right or left edge (short edge) of their strips with the corresponding edges of their papers.

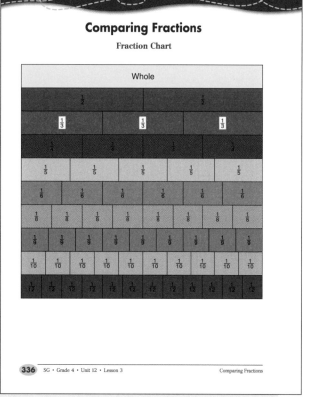

Student Guide - page 336

Once students complete their charts, they can use them to complete the *Comparing Fractions* Activity Pages in the *Student Guide.* A copy of the fraction chart is in the *Student Guide,* but it is smaller than the students' charts. Students need to keep their fraction charts for use as a reference in later lessons of this unit. After students complete the *Comparing Fractions* Activity Pages, provide an opportunity for them to share their work.

Discuss **Question 4** together noting that $\frac{1}{2}$ appears in **Questions 4A–4F.** Point out that $\frac{1}{2}$ is a good benchmark to use when comparing the sizes of different fractions. For example, if you are comparing $\frac{1}{4}$ to $\frac{3}{5}$, you know that $\frac{1}{4}$ is smaller than $\frac{1}{2}$ and $\frac{3}{5}$ is a little larger than $\frac{1}{2}$. Therefore, $\frac{1}{4}$ is smaller than $\frac{3}{5}$. Students can practice using $\frac{1}{2}$ as a benchmark in **Question 5** since each pair of fractions students compare includes one fraction that is equal to or less than $\frac{1}{2}$ and one fraction that is greater than or equal to $\frac{1}{2}$.

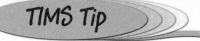

TIMS Tip

If students are not familiar with the symbols for less than (<) and greater than (>), model this before students answer **Question 4.**

Question 7 asks students how to order fractions if they all have the same numerator. Students should see that when all the fractions have the same numerator, you can order them according to their denominators, the larger the denominator the smaller the fraction. Reinforce this concept by having students refer back to their charts.

For **Questions 8–9,** encourage students to use a second strategy to check their answers. For example, students can use $\frac{1}{2}$ as a benchmark to order the fractions in **Question 8A,** then check their work using their fraction charts.

Journal Prompt

Explain why $\frac{1}{2}$ is a good benchmark to use when comparing the sizes of different fractions.

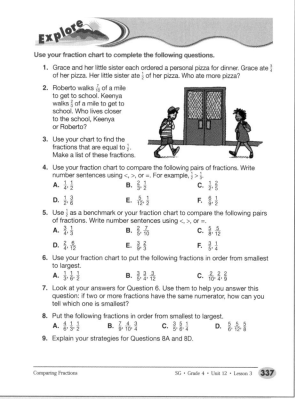

Student Guide - page 337 *(Answers on p. 62)*

Homework and Practice

- Homework *Questions 1–8* on the *Comparing Fractions* Activity Pages can be assigned as homework. Students may use their fraction charts to complete this work.

- DPP Bit I provides practice translating between representations of decimals (diagrams and symbols). Task J provides practice with multidigit multiplication and rounding.

Assessment

- Observe your students as they make and use their fraction charts. Note how well students compare and order fractions. Record your observations on the *Observational Assessment Record*.

- You can also use *Questions 6–8* of the Homework section on the *Comparing Fractions* Activity Pages to assess students' abilities to compare and order fractions.

Homework

Complete the following questions. You may use your fraction chart to help you.

1. Find all the fractions equal to $\frac{1}{4}$ on your chart. Make a list of these fractions.

2. Jackie needs $\frac{5}{8}$ of a yard of fabric for a pillow. Luis needs $\frac{3}{4}$ of a yard of fabric for a banner. Who needs more fabric, Jackie or Luis?

3. Jessie's mom brought a pie to the potluck dinner. It was cut into 6 pieces. Romesh's dad also brought a pie, but it was cut into 12 pieces. At the end of the night, $\frac{1}{6}$ of Jessie's pie was left and $\frac{3}{12}$ of Romesh's pie was left. If the pies were the same size, who had more left-over pie, Jessie's mom or Romesh's dad?

4. Nila practiced her flute for $\frac{1}{2}$ hour on Monday, $\frac{3}{4}$ hour on Tuesday, and $\frac{1}{3}$ hour on Wednesday.
   A. On which day did she practice the longest period of time?
   B. On which day did she practice the shortest period of time?

5. Use your fraction chart to compare the following pairs of fractions. Write a number sentence for each one using <, >, or =.
   A. $\frac{3}{10}, \frac{1}{2}$ B. $\frac{4}{8}, \frac{1}{2}$ C. $\frac{1}{2}, \frac{2}{12}$

6. Use $\frac{1}{2}$ as a benchmark or your fraction chart to compare the following pairs of fractions. Write a number sentence for each one using <, >, or =.
   A. $1, \frac{1}{10}$ B. $\frac{6}{9}, \frac{5}{12}$ C. $\frac{3}{8}, \frac{3}{5}$

7. Use your fraction chart to put the following fractions in order from smallest to largest.
   A. $\frac{4}{8}, \frac{4}{6}, \frac{4}{10}$ B. $\frac{3}{5}, \frac{3}{10}, \frac{3}{8}$ C. $\frac{4}{8}, \frac{4}{12}, \frac{4}{6}$
   D. If two fractions have the same numerator, how can you tell which one is smaller?

8. Put the following fractions in order from smallest to largest. Be prepared to explain your strategies.
   A. $\frac{7}{12}, \frac{1}{3}, \frac{3}{8}$ B. $\frac{3}{5}, \frac{5}{12}, \frac{1}{2}$ C. $\frac{2}{3}, \frac{3}{4}, \frac{1}{6}$
   D. $\frac{1}{5}, \frac{1}{4}, \frac{1}{6}$ E. $\frac{7}{12}, \frac{1}{12}, \frac{5}{12}$ F. $\frac{1}{2}, \frac{3}{4}, \frac{2}{9}$

Student Guide - page 338 *(Answers on p. 63)*

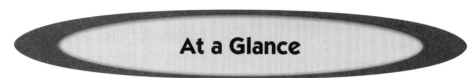

At a Glance

Math Facts and Daily Practice and Problems

DPP Bit I provides practice with decimals. DPP Task J provides practice with multidigit multiplication.

Teaching the Activity

1. Using the *Fraction Strips for the Teacher* Blackline Masters, cut out, color, and mount one set of fraction strips on a chart for demonstration.
2. Students discuss the opening question in the Lesson Guide and share strategies for finding a solution.
3. Students make a fraction chart with their fraction strips by gluing the strips on a piece of paper.
4. Students use their charts to complete *Questions 1–8* on the *Comparing Fractions* Activity Pages in the *Student Guide.*
5. Discuss solutions for *Questions 1–8.*
6. Students keep their charts to use as a reference in later lessons in this unit.

Homework

Assign homework *Questions 1–8* in the *Student Guide.*

Assessment

Use the *Observational Assessment Record* to note students' abilities to order fractions.

Answer Key is on pages 62–63.

Notes:

Fraction Chart

Whole											

| $\frac{1}{2}$ | | | | | | $\frac{1}{2}$ | | | | | |

| $\frac{1}{3}$ | | | | $\frac{1}{3}$ | | | | $\frac{1}{3}$ | | | |

| $\frac{1}{4}$ | | | $\frac{1}{4}$ | | | $\frac{1}{4}$ | | | $\frac{1}{4}$ | | |

| $\frac{1}{5}$ | | $\frac{1}{5}$ | | $\frac{1}{5}$ | | $\frac{1}{5}$ | | $\frac{1}{5}$ | | | |

| $\frac{1}{6}$ | | $\frac{1}{6}$ | | $\frac{1}{6}$ | | $\frac{1}{6}$ | | $\frac{1}{6}$ | | $\frac{1}{6}$ | |

| $\frac{1}{8}$ | $\frac{1}{8}$ | $\frac{1}{8}$ | $\frac{1}{8}$ | $\frac{1}{8}$ | $\frac{1}{8}$ | $\frac{1}{8}$ | $\frac{1}{8}$ | | | | |

| $\frac{1}{9}$ | $\frac{1}{9}$ | $\frac{1}{9}$ | $\frac{1}{9}$ | $\frac{1}{9}$ | $\frac{1}{9}$ | $\frac{1}{9}$ | $\frac{1}{9}$ | $\frac{1}{9}$ | | | |

| $\frac{1}{10}$ | $\frac{1}{10}$ | $\frac{1}{10}$ | $\frac{1}{10}$ | $\frac{1}{10}$ | $\frac{1}{10}$ | $\frac{1}{10}$ | $\frac{1}{10}$ | $\frac{1}{10}$ | $\frac{1}{10}$ | | |

| $\frac{1}{12}$ | $\frac{1}{12}$ | $\frac{1}{12}$ | $\frac{1}{12}$ | $\frac{1}{12}$ | $\frac{1}{12}$ | $\frac{1}{12}$ | $\frac{1}{12}$ | $\frac{1}{12}$ | $\frac{1}{12}$ | $\frac{1}{12}$ | $\frac{1}{12}$ |

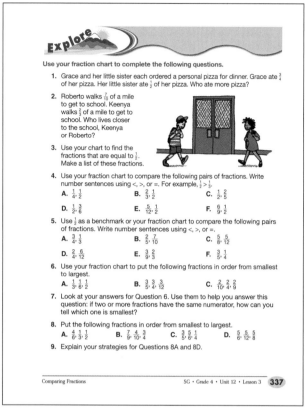

Student Guide - page 337

Student Guide (p. 337)

1. Grace

2. Keenya

3. $\frac{2}{4}, \frac{3}{6}, \frac{4}{8}, \frac{5}{10}, \frac{6}{12}$

4. A. $\frac{1}{4} < \frac{1}{2}$*

   B. $\frac{2}{3} > \frac{1}{2}$

   C. $\frac{1}{2} > \frac{2}{5}$

   D. $\frac{1}{2} = \frac{3}{6}$

   E. $\frac{5}{12} < \frac{1}{2}$

   F. $\frac{6}{9} > \frac{1}{2}$

5. A. $\frac{3}{4} > \frac{1}{3}$*

   B. $\frac{2}{5} < \frac{7}{10}$

   C. $\frac{5}{8} > \frac{5}{12}$

   D. $\frac{2}{4} = \frac{6}{12}$

   E. $\frac{3}{9} < \frac{2}{3}$

   F. $\frac{3}{5} > \frac{1}{4}$

6. A. $\frac{1}{6}, \frac{1}{3}, \frac{1}{2}$

   B. $\frac{3}{12}, \frac{3}{5}, \frac{3}{4}$

   C. $\frac{2}{10}, \frac{2}{9}, \frac{2}{4}$

7. When the numerators are the same, the fraction with the largest denominator is the smallest fraction.*

8. A. $\frac{1}{3}, \frac{1}{2}, \frac{4}{6}$*

   B. $\frac{4}{10}, \frac{3}{4}, \frac{7}{9}$

   C. $\frac{1}{4}, \frac{3}{5}, \frac{5}{6}$

   D. $\frac{5}{12}, \frac{5}{8}, \frac{5}{6}$

9. Possible strategies for **Question 8A:**
   Use a fraction chart. Or, use $\frac{1}{2}$ as a benchmark. $\frac{1}{3}$ is less than $\frac{1}{2}$ and $\frac{4}{6}$ is greater than $\frac{1}{2}$, so $\frac{1}{3} < \frac{1}{2} < \frac{4}{6}$.*

   Possible strategies for **Question 8D:**
   Use a fraction chart. Or, since all the fractions have the same numerator, the fractions with the larger denominators are the smaller fractions so that $\frac{5}{12} < \frac{5}{8} < \frac{5}{6}$.

*Answers and/or discussion are included in the Lesson Guide.

Student Guide (p. 338)

Homework

1. $\frac{2}{8}, \frac{3}{12}$

2. Luis

3. Romesh's dad

4. A. Tuesday

   B. Wednesday

5. A. $\frac{3}{10} < \frac{1}{2}$

   B. $\frac{4}{8} = \frac{1}{2}$

   C. $\frac{1}{2} > \frac{2}{12}$

6. A. $1 > \frac{1}{10}$

   B. $\frac{6}{9} > \frac{5}{12}$

   C. $\frac{3}{8} < \frac{3}{5}$

7. A. $\frac{4}{10}, \frac{4}{8}, \frac{4}{6}$

   B. $\frac{3}{10}, \frac{3}{8}, \frac{3}{5}$

   C. $\frac{4}{12}, \frac{4}{8}, \frac{4}{6}$

   D. When the numerators are the same, the fraction with the larger denominator is the smaller fraction.

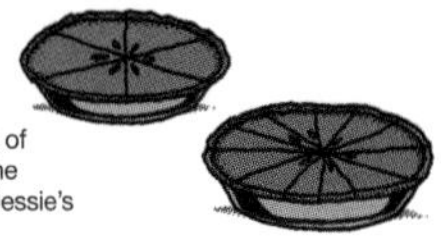

8. A. $\frac{1}{3}, \frac{3}{8}, \frac{7}{12}$

   B. $\frac{5}{12}, \frac{1}{2}, \frac{3}{5}$

   C. $\frac{1}{6}, \frac{2}{3}, \frac{3}{4}$

   D. $\frac{1}{6}, \frac{1}{5}, \frac{1}{4}$

   E. $\frac{1}{12}, \frac{5}{12}, \frac{7}{12}$

   F. $\frac{2}{9}, \frac{1}{2}, \frac{3}{4}$

Student Guide - page 338

Optional Lesson 4

Frabble Game and Bubble Sort

Lesson Overview

Students use a deck of fraction cards to complete two activities. First, students play a game in small groups in which they order fractions according to size by strategically placing cards on the table. Then, in an activity called Bubble Sort, each student holds a fraction card and stands in line. Then, following some simple rules, students rearrange themselves so the cards are in decreasing order.

Key Content

- Comparing and ordering fractions.
- Finding equivalent fractions.

Homework

Students play *Frabble* at home. They should take home a deck of *Frabble* cards, six wild cards, and their *Student Guides.*

Assessment

Use the *Observational Assessment Record* to note students' abilities to compare and order fractions.

Materials List

Supplies and Copies

Student	Teacher
Supplies for Each Student • scissors • envelopes, optional • 1 fraction chart from Lesson 3	**Supplies**
Copies	**Copies/Transparencies** • 1 transparency of *Standard Frabble Cards,* optional (*Discovery Assignment Book* Pages 203–205) • 1 transparency of *Fraction Chart* or fraction chart from Lesson 3 (*Unit Resource Guide* Page 61)

All blackline masters including assessment, transparency, and DPP masters are also on the Teacher Resource CD.

Student Books

Fraction Chart from *Comparing Fractions* (*Student Guide* Page 336)
Frabble Game (*Student Guide* Pages 339–342)
Standard Frabble Cards (*Discovery Assignment Book* Pages 203–205), 1 set per student group
Wild Cards for Frabble (*Discovery Assignment Book* Page 207), 2 cards per student
Challenge Frabble Cards (*Discovery Assignment Book* Page 209), optional

Assessment Tools

Observational Assessment Record (*Unit Resource Guide* Pages 13–14)

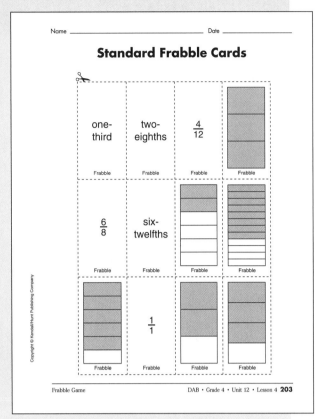

Discovery Assignment Book - page 203

You can play this game in groups of two, three, or four players. Each group needs one deck of 24 *Standard Frabble Cards* from the *Discovery Assignment Book.* Each group cuts out a set of cards before they begin to play or you may make decks of cards and laminate them so the cards will last longer. Each student also needs two wild cards to play this game.

TIMS Tip

Have students store their cards in an envelope when they are not using them. Have students include eight wild cards in their decks so they can play the game at home.

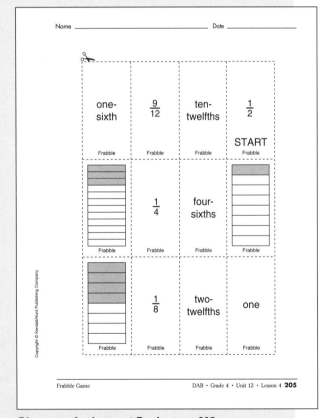

Discovery Assignment Book - page 205

Discovery Assignment Book - page 207

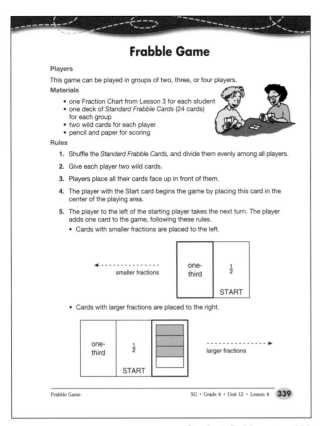

Student Guide - page 339

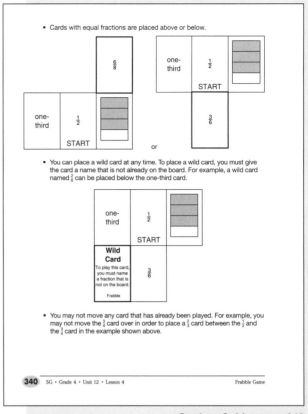

Student Guide - page 340

Teaching the Game

Part 1 Playing Frabble

The game's rules are explained on the *Frabble Game* Game Pages in the *Student Guide*. Discuss the rules using the illustrations in the text or demonstrate them by playing the game on the overhead projector using cards made from transparencies of the *Standard Frabble Cards*.

As students play the game, they will need to decide if one fraction is less than, greater than, or equivalent to other fractions. To help them order fractions, each student should have a fraction chart available. Students may use the fraction chart they made or the Fraction Chart on the *Comparing Fractions* Activity Pages in the *Student Guide* for Lesson 3.

After students play the game with the standard deck of 24 fraction cards and are familiar with both the rules and the strategies, they can make the game more interesting by adding 12 challenge cards. These cards are on the *Challenge Frabble Cards* Game Page in the *Discovery Assignment Book*. The challenge cards add fractions with denominators of fifths and tenths to the standard deck which is limited to fractions with denominators of halves, thirds, fourths, sixths, eighths, and twelfths.

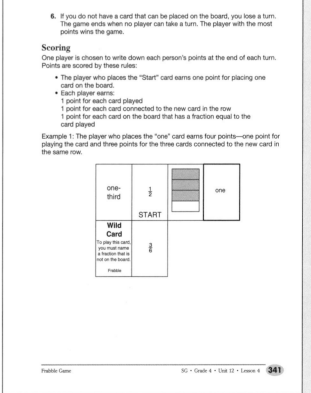

Student Guide - page 341

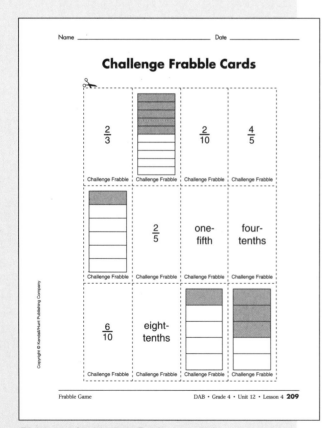

Student Guide - page 342

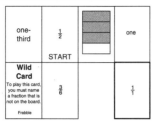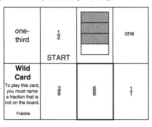

The left column shows Student Guide page 342 content:

Example 2: The player who adds the $\frac{1}{1}$ card earns two points—one point for playing the card ($\frac{1}{1}$) and one point for the equal fraction (one).

one-third	$\frac{1}{2}$ START		one
Wild Card To play this card, you must name a fraction that is not on the board. Frabble	$\frac{3}{6}$		$\frac{1}{1}$

Example 3: The player who adds the $\frac{6}{8}$ card earns a total of five points—one point for the card added ($\frac{6}{8}$); three points for the cards connected in the row (wild card, $\frac{3}{8}$, and $\frac{1}{1}$); and one point for the equal fraction (picture of $\frac{3}{4}$).

one-third	$\frac{1}{2}$ START		one
Wild Card To play this card, you must name a fraction that is not on the board. Frabble	$\frac{3}{6}$	$\frac{6}{8}$	$\frac{1}{1}$

Name _____ Date _____

Challenge Frabble Cards

$\frac{2}{3}$		$\frac{2}{10}$	$\frac{4}{5}$
Challenge Frabble	Challenge Frabble	Challenge Frabble	Challenge Frabble
	$\frac{2}{5}$	one-fifth	four-tenths
Challenge Frabble	Challenge Frabble	Challenge Frabble	Challenge Frabble
$\frac{6}{10}$	eight-tenths		
Challenge Frabble	Challenge Frabble	Challenge Frabble	Challenge Frabble

Frabble Game   DAB • Grade 4 • Unit 12 • Lesson 4 **209**

Discovery Assignment Book - page 209

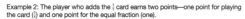

TIMS Tip

Each group of students playing a game needs a scorekeeper. You can make up a rule to determine which player will serve as the scorekeeper first, such as "the child in each group whose name comes first (or last) alphabetically" or "the student on the east side of the table."

Part 2   Bubble Sort

Pass out a *Frabble* card randomly to each student and then ask the class to form one line. Tell students they will follow a procedure called Bubble Sort that will sort the cards from largest to smallest. Designate the head of the line as the home of the largest number and the other end of the line as the home of the smallest number. The object of the sort is for the largest fractions to "bubble up" to the head of the line.

TIMS Tip

Demonstrate the bubble sort to the class with five students before the whole class begins the sort.

To bubble sort:

- Ask the first two students at the head of the line to compare the fractions on their cards. If the smaller fraction is at the head of the line, then the students switch places. If the larger fraction is already at the head of the line or if the fractions are equivalent, the students stay in their original places.
- Then, the second and third students in line compare their fractions, switching places so that the larger fraction moves toward the head of the line.
- Continue with the students currently standing in the third and fourth places and then with the remaining students in the line until all adjacent pairs have compared and ordered their two fractions.

Note that students change places, they do not trade cards, and they may only switch places with a student standing to the left or right of them.

Once you reach the end of the line, ask students to read the fractions on their cards out loud. Ask

- *Are all the fractions in order?*

After one pass through the line, it is not likely that the fractions will be in order, so the process is repeated. Once students understand the procedure, speed up the ordering process by having adjacent pairs of students compare their fractions simultaneously and switch places as necessary. Remind students that they may only switch places with a student standing to the left or right of them.

Continue until no more switches can be made. Then, ask students to read off the numbers as a final check to see that the fractions are in order.

Homework and Practice

Students play *Frabble* with their families. Each student needs to take home a deck of *Frabble* cards, six wild cards, and his or her *Student Guide*.

Assessment

- As students play the game, look for students' abilities to order fractions correctly. Record your observations on the *Observational Assessment Record*.

- Choose five of the *Frabble* cards (such as $1, \frac{1}{8}, \frac{1}{2}$, a picture of $\frac{1}{6}$, and four-sixths) and ask students to place them in order on their desks. Students can write the order of the cards on a sheet of paper or you can make a visual check. Record students' abilities to compare and order fractions on the *Observational Assessment Record*.

Extension

Use the *Frabble* cards to play Frabble War. This is a game for two players. Each student begins with half of the deck placed in a pile face down in front of him or her. Each player turns over the top card from his or her pile. Whoever has the greater fraction showing wins the two cards. If the two fractions are equivalent, then each player turns over another card. Whoever has the greater fraction wins all four cards. If there is another tie, then players turn over two more cards, continuing the process until they break the tie. The player with the larger fraction wins all the cards in the "war." Students may play the cards they win. Play for 10 minutes or until one player runs out of cards. The player with the most cards at the end of the game is the winner.

Challenge students to make up a card game using the *Frabble* cards.

Content Note

Bubble Sort. The bubble sort demonstrates an algorithm computer programmers sometimes use to order numbers or words in a list. The name comes from the image of bubbles in water bubbling up to the surface. There are faster sorting schemes, but this one works well in a classroom. You may wish to start the sort by designating one student (or yourself) as the computer. During the first or second pass through the line, the computer looks at each pair of adjacent fractions and decides if students holding the cards should switch places or not. This will go slowly and students will soon want to make the comparisons simultaneously.

Before the Game

Make decks of *Standard Frabble Cards* from the *Discovery Assignment Book*. Each group will need one deck. Each student will also need two wild cards. Prepare Challenge cards to add to the deck after students are comfortable with the rules.

Part 1. Playing Frabble

1. Discuss the rules of the game using the illustrations in the *Student Guide* or transparencies of *Standard Frabble Cards*.
2. Students play the game in groups of 2, 3, or 4 using one deck of *Standard Frabble Cards* and keeping score with pencil and paper.
3. When students are familiar with the game's rules and strategies, groups can add the *Challenge Frabble Cards* to the deck.

Part 2. Bubble Sort

1. Each student stands in a line holding a *Frabble* card.
2. Designate the head of the line as the home for the largest fraction on the cards and the other end of the line as the home for the smallest fraction.
3. Students compare the fractions on their cards with the fractions on the cards of the students standing on either side of them. Moving toward the head of the line, a student with the larger fraction trades places with the student with the smaller fraction. Students continue comparing fractions and trading places with students immediately next to them when appropriate until all the fractions are in order from largest to smallest.

Homework

Students play *Frabble* at home. They should take home a deck of *Frabble* cards, six wild cards, and their *Student Guides*.

Assessment

Use the *Observational Assessment Record* to note students' abilities to compare and order fractions.

Extension

1. Use the *Frabble* cards to play *Frabble War*.
2. Challenge students to make up a card game using the *Frabble* cards.

Notes:

Lesson 5

Equivalent Fractions

Lesson Overview

Students find equivalent fractions using their fraction charts from Lesson 3, write number sentences to represent the equivalent fractions, and look for patterns in the number sentences. They use these patterns to write an equivalent fraction for a given fraction.

Key Content
- Finding equivalent fractions.

Key Vocabulary
- equivalent fractions

Math Facts
Use DPP items K and L to practice multiplication and division facts as students build number sense.

Homework
Assign the Homework section on the *Equivalent Fractions* Activity Pages in the *Student Guide*. Students will need their fraction charts to complete this assignment.

Assessment
1. Use the *Observational Assessment Record* to note students' abilities to find equivalent fractions.
2. Use Home Practice Part 3 as an assessment.

Materials List

Supplies and Copies

Student	Teacher
Supplies for Each Student • 1 fraction chart from Lesson 3	**Supplies**
Copies	**Copies/Transparencies**

All blackline masters including assessment, transparency, and DPP masters are also on the Teacher Resource CD.

Student Books

Equivalent Fractions (*Student Guide* Pages 343–345)
Fraction Chart from *Comparing Fractions* (*Student Guide* Page 336)

Daily Practice and Problems and Home Practice

DPP items K–L (*Unit Resource Guide* Page 21)
Home Practice Part 3 (*Discovery Assignment Book* Page 194)

Note: Classrooms whose pacing differs significantly from the suggested pacing of the units should use the Math Facts Calendar in Section 4 of the *Facts Resource Guide* to ensure students receive the complete math facts program.

Assessment Tools

Observational Assessment Record (*Unit Resource Guide* Pages 13–14)

Daily Practice and Problems

Suggestions for using the DPPs are on page 76.

K. Bit: More Division Fact Practice
(URG p. 21)

Find the number *n* that makes each sentence true.

A. $54 \div n = 9$ B. $720 \div n = 90$
C. $n \times 400 = 36,000$ D. $70 \times n = 63,000$
E. $90 \times n = 450$ F. $n \div 9 = 300$

L. Task: Fact Practice (URG p. 21)

A. $30 \times 90 =$ B. $630 \div 70 =$
C. $360 \div 9 =$ D. $90 \times 80 =$
E. $2700 \div 9 =$ F. $9000 \times 90 =$
G. $54,000 \div 9 =$ H. $1800 \div 90 =$
I. $900 \times 0 =$ J. $900 \div 90 =$

Teaching the Activity

The first part of this lesson is a teacher-led activity in which students look at equivalent fractions using their fraction charts from Lesson 3. Students look for patterns and use these patterns to find equivalent fractions not shown on their charts.

Begin this lesson by putting the fraction $\frac{1}{2}$ on the board or on a blank overhead transparency. Ask students to look at their fraction charts and find all the fractions that are equivalent to $\frac{1}{2}$. List these on the board as shown in Figure 13. Explain that fractions with the same value are called **equivalent fractions.**

Use these discussion prompts to explore these equivalent fractions:

- *Compare the denominators of each of these fractions. What do you notice? (*Students should see that the denominators are all even numbers and therefore all multiples of two.)

- *Compare the numerator and the denominator in each fraction. What do you see?* (When a fraction is equivalent to $\frac{1}{2}$ the numerator is half the value of the denominator.)

- *Is $\frac{20}{40}$ equivalent to $\frac{1}{2}$?* (Since 40 is a multiple of 2 and since 20 is half of 40, then $\frac{20}{40} = \frac{1}{2}$.)

- *Suggest other fractions that are equivalent to $\frac{1}{2}$.* (Evaluate each student suggestion, adding those that are appropriate to the list of equivalent fractions.)

Write the following number sentences on the board: $\frac{1}{2} = \frac{2}{4}$, $\frac{1}{2} = \frac{4}{8}$, $\frac{1}{2} = \frac{5}{10}$, $\frac{1}{2} = \frac{6}{12}$, $\frac{1}{2} = \frac{20}{40}$, and some of the fractions suggested by the students. Ask:

- *Look for a pattern in these number sentences by first comparing the numerators of the fractions in each sentence and then the denominators.*

Students may express the patterns in many ways, but they should see that if you multiply (or divide) both the numerator and the denominator of a fraction by the same number the result will be an equivalent fraction. Figure 14 shows this pattern.

$$\frac{1}{2} = \frac{2}{4} = \frac{3}{6} = \frac{4}{8} = \frac{5}{10} = \frac{6}{12}$$

Figure 13: *Fractions that are equivalent to $\frac{1}{2}$*

$$\frac{1}{2} = \frac{1 \times 5}{2 \times 5} = \frac{5}{10} \qquad \frac{6}{12} = \frac{6 \div 6}{12 \div 6} = \frac{1}{2}$$

Figure 14: *Equivalent fractions*

$$\frac{3}{4} = \frac{3 \times \square}{4 \times \square} = \frac{6}{8} \qquad \frac{3}{4} = \frac{3 \times \square}{4 \times \square} = \frac{9}{12}$$

$$\frac{1}{3} = \frac{1 \times \square}{3 \times \square} = \frac{2}{6} \qquad \frac{1}{3} = \frac{1 \times \square}{3 \times \square} = \frac{4}{12}$$

$$\frac{2}{5} = \frac{2 \times \square}{5 \times \square} = \frac{4}{10}$$

Figure 15: *Equivalent fractions*

Continue this lesson by asking students to use their fraction charts to suggest number sentences for those fractions that are equivalent to $\frac{3}{4}$, $\frac{1}{3}$, and $\frac{2}{5}$. Write these on the board or overhead as shown in Figure 15. Using the pattern found earlier, ask:

* *What number should I multiply both the numerator and denominator by to find the equivalent fraction?*

Once students complete this task, ask them to suggest other fractions that are equivalent to $\frac{3}{4}$, $\frac{1}{3}$, and $\frac{2}{5}$. Add these fractions to the board by writing the appropriate number sentences. For example, students may suggest the following number sentences for $\frac{3}{4}$: $\frac{3}{4} = \frac{30}{40}$ and $\frac{3}{4} = \frac{300}{400}$. As students suggest number sentences, ask them to explain how they found the equivalent fractions.

Once students are comfortable using multiplication to find equivalent fractions, put the following number sentences on the board:

$$\frac{?}{3} = \frac{4}{6} \qquad \frac{10}{12} = \frac{?}{6} \qquad \frac{6}{10} = \frac{3}{?} \qquad \frac{?}{4} = \frac{2}{8}$$

Ask students to find the missing numerators and denominators. Students should share the strategies they use. Students may suggest using multiplication as a strategy. For example, to find the missing number in the sentence $\frac{?}{3} = \frac{4}{6}$, students may say: "Since you multiply 3 by 2 in order to get the denominator of 6, what number would you multiply by 2 in order to get the numerator of 4? Since 2 times 2 equals 4, the missing numerator is 2." Other students may suggest using division as a strategy. For example, in the number sentence $\frac{10}{12} = \frac{?}{6}$, they may say, "Since you divide 12 by 2 in order to get 6, you must also divide 10 by 2. This gives a numerator of 5."

Continue this lesson by having students use the *Equivalent Fractions* Activity Pages in the *Student Guide.* The short vignette reviews the concepts completed in class. After reviewing the vignette, students can complete *Questions 1–6.* These questions can be completed with a partner or students can work independently and then check their work with another student. Provide an opportunity for students to share their answers and strategies.

Discuss *Questions 3–4.* For *Question 3A* students use their fraction charts to find that $\frac{1}{3}$, $\frac{2}{6}$, and $\frac{4}{12}$ are equivalent to $\frac{3}{9}$. Write $\frac{3}{9} = \frac{2}{6}$ on the board. Point out that nine is not a multiple of six. Ask:

- *How do you know that $\frac{3}{9}$ is equal to $\frac{2}{6}$?* (The fraction strips for $\frac{3}{9}$ and $\frac{2}{6}$ are the same length. $\frac{3}{9}$ and $\frac{2}{6}$ are both equal to $\frac{1}{3}$.)

- *How do you know that $\frac{3}{9}$ is equal to $\frac{4}{12}$?* (The fraction strips for $\frac{3}{9}$ and $\frac{4}{12}$ are the same length. $\frac{3}{9}$ and $\frac{4}{12}$ are both equal to $\frac{1}{3}$.)

Question 4 asks students to complete the number sentence $\frac{6}{12} = \frac{?}{8}$. Since students cannot multiply numerator and denominator by the same whole number to find an equivalent fraction, they must use another strategy. Students can use their fraction charts to show that the length of the $\frac{6}{12}$ fraction strip is the same length as the $\frac{4}{8}$ fraction strip. Or, they can use the fact that $\frac{6}{12}$ and $\frac{4}{8}$ are both equal to $\frac{1}{2}$.

Content Note

Equivalent Fractions. In mathematics, two fractions that have the same value are considered equivalent fractions. At this level of mathematics, we do not distinguish between the words equal and equivalent. Therefore, it is acceptable for students to use either equal or equivalent when comparing two fractions that have the same value.

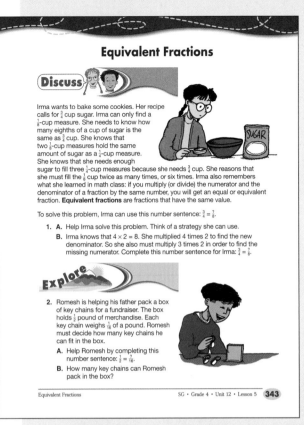

Equivalent Fractions

Discuss

Irma wants to bake some cookies. Her recipe calls for $\frac{3}{4}$ cup sugar. Irma can only find a $\frac{1}{8}$-cup measure. She needs to know how many eighths of a cup of sugar is the same as $\frac{3}{4}$ cup. She knows that two $\frac{1}{8}$-cup measures hold the same amount of sugar as a $\frac{1}{4}$-cup measure. She knows that she needs enough sugar to fill three $\frac{1}{4}$-cup measures because she needs $\frac{3}{4}$ cup. She reasons that she must fill the $\frac{1}{8}$ cup twice as many times, or six times. Irma also remembers what she learned in math class: if you multiply (or divide) the numerator and the denominator of a fraction by the same number, you will get an equal or equivalent fraction. **Equivalent fractions** are fractions that have the same value.

To solve this problem, Irma can use this number sentence: $\frac{3}{4} = \frac{?}{8}$.

1. **A.** Help Irma solve this problem. Think of a strategy she can use.
   B. Irma knows that $4 \times 2 = 8$. She multiplied 4 times 2 to find the new denominator. So she also must multiply 3 times 2 in order to find the missing numerator. Complete this number sentence for Irma: $\frac{3}{4} = \frac{?}{8}$.

Explore

2. Romesh is helping his father pack a box of key chains for a fundraiser. The box holds $\frac{1}{2}$ pound of merchandise. Each key chain weighs $\frac{1}{16}$ of a pound. Romesh must decide how many key chains he can fit in the box.
   A. Help Romesh by completing this number sentence: $\frac{1}{2} = \frac{?}{16}$.
   B. How many key chains can Romesh pack in the box?

Equivalent Fractions   SG • Grade 4 • Unit 12 • Lesson 5   **343**

Student Guide - page 343 (Answers on p. 78)

3. **A.** Use your fraction chart to find three fractions that are equivalent to $\frac{3}{8}$. Write number sentences to record the equivalent fractions.
   B. Find three other fractions that are equivalent to $\frac{3}{8}$. Write number sentences to record the equivalent fractions.
   C. Explain the strategy you used to find the equivalent fractions.
4. Complete the number sentence: $\frac{4}{8} = \frac{?}{12}$. Explain how you know.
5. **A.** Use your fraction chart to find a fraction that is equivalent to $\frac{2}{3}$. Write a number sentence to record the equivalent fractions.
   B. Find three other fractions that are equivalent to $\frac{2}{3}$. Write number sentences to record the equivalent fractions.
   C. Explain the strategy you used to find the equivalent fractions.
6. Complete the number sentences below. Use your fraction chart.
   A. $\frac{3}{4} = \frac{?}{8}$ **B.** $\frac{1}{2} = \frac{?}{10}$ **C.** $\frac{2}{3} = \frac{?}{9}$ **D.** $\frac{6}{9} = \frac{?}{12}$
   E. $\frac{1}{2} = \frac{4}{?}$ **F.** $\frac{6}{10} = \frac{?}{5}$ **G.** $\frac{8}{12} = \frac{?}{?}$ **H.** $\frac{3}{12} = \frac{?}{8}$

Homework

1. Complete the number sentences to make each fraction equivalent to $\frac{1}{2}$.
   A. $\frac{1}{2} = \frac{3}{?}$ **B.** $\frac{1}{2} = \frac{?}{18}$ **C.** $\frac{1}{2} = \frac{12}{?}$
   D. $\frac{1}{2} = \frac{?}{60}$ **E.** $\frac{1}{2} = \frac{50}{?}$ **F.** $\frac{1}{2} = \frac{?}{7}$
2. Write 5 fractions equivalent to $\frac{2}{3}$.
3. Romesh is packing a box filled with plastic cars for his father. The box holds $\frac{3}{4}$ pound of merchandise. Each plastic car weighs $\frac{1}{16}$ pound.
   A. Complete this number sentence to help Romesh decide how many sixteenths of a pound is equivalent to $\frac{3}{4}$ pound. $\frac{3}{4} = \frac{?}{16}$.
   B. How many plastic cars can Romesh pack in the box?
   C. What is another name for $\frac{4}{16}$ of a pound?

344   SG • Grade 4 • Unit 12 • Lesson 5   Equivalent Fractions

Student Guide - page 344 (Answers on p. 78)

4. Write 5 fractions equivalent to $\frac{2}{5}$.

5. Shannon wants to purchase $\frac{1}{3}$ yard of ribbon. There are 36 inches in a yard.
  A. Complete the following number sentence to help the clerk decide how many inches of ribbon she must cut: $\frac{1}{3} = \frac{?}{36}$.
  B. How many inches of ribbon should she cut?

6. Use the Fraction Chart to complete the number sentence: $\frac{6}{8} = \frac{?}{12}$.

Complete the following number sentences.

7. $\frac{1}{2} = \frac{?}{12}$ **8.** $\frac{3}{4} = \frac{?}{16}$ **9.** $\frac{4}{6} = \frac{?}{9}$

10. $\frac{3}{5} = \frac{?}{20}$ **11.** $\frac{10}{16} = \frac{?}{8}$ **12.** $\frac{8}{24} = \frac{?}{3}$

13. $\frac{10}{15} = \frac{?}{3}$ **14.** $\frac{1}{5} = \frac{?}{100}$ **15.** $\frac{1}{5} = \frac{?}{20}$

16. $\frac{75}{100} = \frac{?}{4}$ **17.** $\frac{2}{4} = \frac{?}{6}$ **18.** $\frac{20}{24} = \frac{5}{?}$

Use <, >, or = to write number sentences to compare the following pairs of numbers.

19. $\frac{5}{9}, \frac{1}{2}$ **20.** $\frac{3}{4}, \frac{30}{40}$ **21.** $\frac{72}{100}, \frac{7}{10}$

Equivalent Fractions   SG • Grade 4 • Unit 12 • Lesson 5   **345**

Student Guide - page 345 *(Answers on p. 79)*

Name _____ Date _____

PART 3 Fraction Chart
Use the fraction chart you created in Lesson 3 or the Fraction Chart in your *Student Guide* in Lesson 3.

1. Order these fractions from smallest to largest.
  A. $\frac{2}{3}$ $\frac{1}{4}$ $\frac{5}{6}$ $\frac{3}{8}$ $\frac{2}{12}$ _____
  B. $\frac{3}{5}$ $\frac{1}{8}$ $\frac{4}{9}$ $\frac{1}{10}$ $\frac{1}{2}$ _____

2. Find one or two equivalent fractions for each of the following.
  A. $\frac{6}{8}$ **B.** $\frac{3}{9}$ **C.** $\frac{2}{3}$ **D.** $\frac{4}{10}$

  E. $\frac{3}{5}$ **F.** $\frac{3}{12}$ **G.** $\frac{6}{12}$ **H.** $\frac{1}{5}$

3. Complete the number sentences.
  A. $\frac{5}{6} = \frac{?}{12}$ **B.** $\frac{8}{10} = \frac{4}{?}$ **C.** $\frac{4}{5} = \frac{?}{20}$

4. Name a fraction smaller than each of the following.
  A. $\frac{1}{2}$ **B.** $\frac{1}{4}$ **C.** $\frac{3}{5}$ **D.** $\frac{7}{8}$

5. Name a fraction greater than each of the following. Do not name a fraction equivalent to 1.
  A. $\frac{1}{2}$ **B.** $\frac{3}{4}$ **C.** $\frac{1}{6}$ **D.** $\frac{9}{10}$

194 DAB • Grade 4 • Unit 12   EXPLORING FRACTIONS

Discovery Assignment Book - page 194 *(Answers on p. 79)*

Math Facts

DPP items K and L provide practice with math facts using numbers ending with zeros.

Homework and Practice

Assign the Homework section of the *Equivalent Fractions* Activity Pages in the *Student Guide*. Students will need their fraction charts.

Assessment

• Use the *Observational Assessment Record* to note students' progress finding equivalent fractions.

• Use Part 3 of the Home Practice to assess students' abilities to order fractions and find equivalent fractions.

Answers for the Home Practice Part 3 are in the Answer Key at the end of this lesson and at the end of this unit.

At a Glance

Math Facts and Daily Practice and Problems

Use DPP items K and L to practice multiplication and division facts as students build number sense.

Teaching the Activity

1. Ask students to use their fraction chart from Lesson 3 to find all the fractions equivalent to $\frac{1}{2}$. List these on the board or overhead.
2. Ask students to compare the numerators and the denominators of the equivalent fractions to look for patterns.
3. Ask students to suggest other fractions equivalent to $\frac{1}{2}$.
4. Write number sentences on the board or overhead showing the equivalencies.
5. Students look for patterns in the number sentences.
6. Students use the patterns (multiplying or dividing the numerator and the denominator by the same number) to find fractions equivalent to $\frac{3}{4}$, $\frac{1}{3}$, and $\frac{2}{5}$.
7. Students use the patterns to complete number sentences involving equivalent fractions.
8. Students complete *Questions 1–6* on the *Equivalent Fractions* Activity Pages.
9. Discuss *Questions 3* and *4* as a class.

Homework

Assign the Homework section on the *Equivalent Fractions* Activity Pages in the *Student Guide.* Students will need their fraction charts to complete this assignment.

Assessment

1. Use the *Observational Assessment Record* to note students' abilities to find equivalent fractions.
2. Use Home Practice Part 3 as an assessment.

Answer Key is on pages 78–79.

Notes:

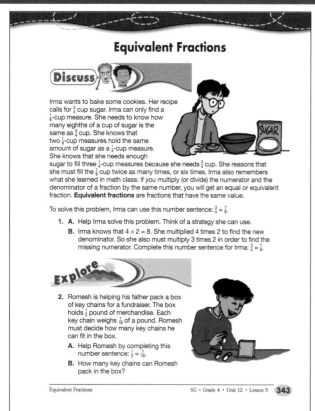

Equivalent Fractions

Discuss

Irma wants to bake some cookies. Her recipe calls for $\frac{3}{4}$ cup sugar. Irma can only find a $\frac{1}{8}$-cup measure. She needs to know how many eighths of a cup of sugar is the same as $\frac{3}{4}$ cup. She knows that two $\frac{1}{8}$-cup measures hold the same amount of sugar as a $\frac{1}{4}$-cup measure. She knows that she needs enough sugar to fill three $\frac{1}{4}$-cup measures because she needs $\frac{3}{4}$ cup. She reasons that she must fill the $\frac{1}{8}$ cup twice as many times, or six times. Irma also remembers what she learned in math class: if you multiply (or divide) the numerator and the denominator of a fraction by the same number, you will get an equal or equivalent fraction. **Equivalent fractions** are fractions that have the same value.

To solve this problem, Irma can use this number sentence: $\frac{3}{4} = \frac{?}{8}$.

1. **A.** Help Irma solve this problem. Think of a strategy she can use.
   B. Irma knows that $4 \times 2 = 8$. She multiplied 4 times 2 to find the new denominator. So she also must multiply 3 times 2 in order to find the missing numerator. Complete this number sentence for Irma: $\frac{3}{4} = \frac{?}{8}$.

Explore

2. Romesh is helping his father pack a box of key chains for a fundraiser. The box holds $\frac{1}{2}$ pound of merchandise. Each key chain weighs $\frac{1}{16}$ of a pound. Romesh must decide how many key chains he can fit in the box.
   A. Help Romesh by completing this number sentence: $\frac{1}{2} = \frac{?}{16}$.
   B. How many key chains can Romesh pack in the box?

Equivalent Fractions   SG • Grade 4 • Unit 12 • Lesson 5   **343**

Student Guide - page 343

---

3. **A.** Use your fraction chart to find three fractions that are equivalent to $\frac{2}{3}$. Write number sentences to record the equivalent fractions.
   B. Find three other fractions that are equivalent to $\frac{1}{3}$. Write number sentences to record the equivalent fractions.
   C. Explain the strategy you used to find the equivalent fractions.
4. Complete the number sentence: $\frac{4}{8} = \frac{?}{12}$. Explain how you know.
5. **A.** Use your fraction chart to find a fraction that is equivalent to $\frac{3}{5}$. Write a number sentence to record the equivalent fractions.
   B. Find three other fractions that are equivalent to $\frac{3}{5}$. Write number sentences to record the equivalent fractions.
   C. Explain the strategy you used to find the equivalent fractions.
6. Complete the number sentences below. Use your fraction chart.
   A. $\frac{3}{4} = \frac{?}{8}$ **B.** $\frac{1}{2} = \frac{?}{10}$ **C.** $\frac{2}{3} = \frac{?}{9}$ **D.** $\frac{6}{9} = \frac{?}{12}$
   E. $\frac{1}{2} = \frac{4}{?}$ **F.** $\frac{6}{10} = \frac{?}{5}$ **G.** $\frac{8}{12} = \frac{?}{3}$ **H.** $\frac{3}{12} = \frac{?}{8}$

Homework

1. Complete the number sentences to make each fraction equivalent to $\frac{1}{2}$.
   A. $\frac{1}{2} = \frac{3}{?}$ **B.** $\frac{1}{2} = \frac{?}{18}$ **C.** $\frac{1}{2} = \frac{12}{?}$
   D. $\frac{1}{2} = \frac{?}{60}$ **E.** $\frac{1}{2} = \frac{50}{?}$ **F.** $\frac{1}{2} = \frac{?}{?}$
2. Write 5 fractions equivalent to $\frac{2}{3}$.
3. Romesh is packing a box filled with plastic cars for his father. The box holds $\frac{3}{4}$ pound of merchandise. Each plastic car weighs $\frac{1}{16}$ pound.
   A. Complete this number sentence to help Romesh decide how many sixteenths of a pound is equivalent to $\frac{3}{4}$ pound. $\frac{3}{4} = \frac{?}{16}$.
   B. How many plastic cars can Romesh pack in the box?
   C. What is another name for $\frac{1}{16}$ of a pound?

344 SG • Grade 4 • Unit 12 • Lesson 5   Equivalent Fractions

Student Guide - page 344

Student Guide (pp. 343–344)

Equivalent Fractions

1. **A.** Since multiplying the denominator (4) times 2 gives the denominator of the second fraction, multiply the numerator (3) by 2 to get the numerator (6) of the equivalent fraction.

   B. $\frac{3}{4} = \frac{6}{8}$

2. **A.** $\frac{1}{2} = \frac{8}{16}$

   B. 8 key chains

3. **A.** $\frac{3}{9} = \frac{1}{3} = \frac{2}{6} = \frac{4}{12}$

   B. $\frac{3}{9} = \frac{6}{18} = \frac{9}{27} = \frac{12}{36}$ (Answers will vary.)

   C. Multiply (or divide) numerator and denominator by the same number or use the Fraction Chart.

4. $\frac{4}{8} = \frac{6}{12}$. Explanations will vary. Possible explanations: The fraction strip for $\frac{4}{8}$ is the same length as the fraction strip for $\frac{6}{12}$. Or, I know that $\frac{4}{8}$ and $\frac{6}{12}$ both equal $\frac{1}{2}$.

5. **A.** $\frac{3}{5} = \frac{6}{10}$

   B. $\frac{3}{5} = \frac{9}{15} = \frac{12}{20} = \frac{15}{25}$ (Answers will vary.)

   C. Multiply numerator and denominator by the same number.

6. **A.** $\frac{3}{4} = \frac{6}{8}$ **B.** $\frac{1}{2} = \frac{5}{10}$

   C. $\frac{2}{3} = \frac{6}{9}$ **D.** $\frac{6}{9} = \frac{8}{12}$

   E. $\frac{1}{2} = \frac{4}{8}$ **F.** $\frac{6}{10} = \frac{3}{5}$

   G. $\frac{8}{12} = \frac{2}{3}$ **H.** $\frac{3}{12} = \frac{2}{8}$

Homework

1. **A.** $\frac{1}{2} = \frac{3}{6}$

   B. $\frac{1}{2} = \frac{9}{18}$

   C. $\frac{1}{2} = \frac{12}{24}$

   D. $\frac{1}{2} = \frac{30}{60}$

   E. $\frac{1}{2} = \frac{50}{100}$

   F. Answers will vary.

2. $\frac{2}{3} = \frac{4}{6} = \frac{6}{9} = \frac{8}{12} = \frac{10}{15} = \frac{12}{18}$ (Answers will vary.)

3. **A.** $\frac{3}{4} = \frac{12}{16}$

   B. 12 cars

   C. an ounce

Student Guide (p. 345)

4. $\frac{2}{5} = \frac{4}{10} = \frac{6}{15} = \frac{8}{20} = \frac{10}{25} = \frac{12}{30}$ (Answers will vary.)

5. A. $\frac{1}{3} = \frac{12}{36}$

B. 12 inches

6. $\frac{6}{8} = \frac{9}{12}$ **7.** $\frac{1}{2} = \frac{6}{12}$

8. $\frac{3}{4} = \frac{12}{16}$ **9.** $\frac{4}{6} = \frac{6}{9}$

10. $\frac{3}{5} = \frac{12}{20}$ **11.** $\frac{10}{16} = \frac{5}{8}$

12. $\frac{8}{24} = \frac{1}{3}$ **13.** $\frac{10}{15} = \frac{2}{3}$

14. $\frac{1}{5} = \frac{20}{100}$ **15.** $\frac{1}{5} = \frac{4}{20}$

16. $\frac{75}{100} = \frac{3}{4}$ **17.** $\frac{2}{4} = \frac{3}{6}$

18. $\frac{20}{24} = \frac{5}{6}$ **19.** $\frac{5}{9} > \frac{1}{2}$

20. $\frac{3}{4} = \frac{30}{40}$ **21.** $\frac{72}{100} > \frac{7}{10}$

4. Write 5 fractions equivalent to $\frac{2}{5}$.

5. Shannon wants to purchase $\frac{1}{3}$ yard of ribbon. There are 36 inches in a yard.
   A. Complete the following number sentence to help the clerk decide how many inches of ribbon she must cut: $\frac{1}{3} = \frac{?}{36}$.
   B. How many inches of ribbon should she cut?

6. Use the Fraction Chart to complete the number sentence: $\frac{6}{8} = \frac{?}{12}$.

Complete the following number sentences.

7. $\frac{1}{2} = \frac{?}{12}$ 8. $\frac{3}{4} = \frac{?}{16}$ 9. $\frac{4}{6} = \frac{?}{9}$

10. $\frac{3}{5} = \frac{?}{20}$ 11. $\frac{10}{16} = \frac{?}{8}$ 12. $\frac{8}{24} = \frac{?}{3}$

13. $\frac{10}{15} = \frac{?}{3}$ 14. $\frac{1}{5} = \frac{?}{100}$ 15. $\frac{1}{5} = \frac{?}{20}$

16. $\frac{75}{100} = \frac{?}{4}$ 17. $\frac{2}{4} = \frac{?}{6}$ 18. $\frac{20}{24} = \frac{5}{?}$

Use <, >, or = to write number sentences to compare the following pairs of numbers.

19. $\frac{5}{9}, \frac{1}{2}$ 20. $\frac{3}{4}, \frac{30}{40}$ 21. $\frac{72}{100}, \frac{7}{10}$

Equivalent Fractions   SG · Grade 4 · Unit 12 · Lesson 5   **345**

Student Guide - page 345

Discovery Assignment Book (p. 194)

Home Practice*

Part 3. Fraction Chart

1. A. $\frac{2}{12}, \frac{1}{4}, \frac{3}{8}, \frac{2}{3}, \frac{5}{6}$

B. $\frac{1}{10}, \frac{1}{8}, \frac{4}{9}, \frac{1}{2}, \frac{3}{5}$

2. Answers will vary. Students name 1 or 2 equivalent fractions for each letter.

A. $\frac{3}{4}, \frac{9}{12}$ **B.** $\frac{1}{3}, \frac{4}{12}$

C. $\frac{4}{6}, \frac{6}{9}, \frac{8}{12}$ **D.** $\frac{2}{5}$

E. $\frac{6}{10}$ **F.** $\frac{1}{4}, \frac{2}{8}$

G. $\frac{1}{2}, \frac{2}{4}, \frac{3}{6}, \frac{4}{8}, \frac{5}{10}$ **H.** $\frac{2}{10}$

3. A. $\frac{5}{6} = \frac{10}{12}$

B. $\frac{8}{10} = \frac{4}{5}$

C. $\frac{4}{5} = \frac{16}{20}$

4. Answers will vary.

5. Answers will vary.

Name _____ Date _____

PART 3 **Fraction Chart**
Use the fraction chart you created in Lesson 3 or the Fraction Chart in your *Student Guide* in Lesson 3.

1. Order these fractions from smallest to largest.
   A. $\frac{2}{3} \quad \frac{1}{4} \quad \frac{5}{6} \quad \frac{3}{8} \quad \frac{2}{12}$ _____
   B. $\frac{3}{5} \quad \frac{1}{8} \quad \frac{4}{9} \quad \frac{1}{10} \quad \frac{1}{2}$ _____

2. Find one or two equivalent fractions for each of the following.
   A. $\frac{6}{8}$ B. $\frac{3}{9}$ C. $\frac{2}{3}$ D. $\frac{4}{10}$

   E. $\frac{3}{5}$ F. $\frac{3}{12}$ G. $\frac{6}{12}$ H. $\frac{1}{5}$

3. Complete the number sentences.
   A. $\frac{5}{6} = \frac{?}{12}$ B. $\frac{8}{10} = \frac{4}{?}$ C. $\frac{4}{5} = \frac{?}{20}$

4. Name a fraction smaller than each of the following.
   A. $\frac{1}{2}$ B. $\frac{1}{4}$ C. $\frac{3}{5}$ D. $\frac{7}{8}$

5. Name a fraction greater than each of the following. Do not name a fraction equivalent to 1.
   A. $\frac{1}{2}$ B. $\frac{3}{4}$ C. $\frac{1}{6}$ D. $\frac{9}{10}$

194 DAB · Grade 4 · Unit 12   EXPLORING FRACTIONS

Discovery Assignment Book - page 194

*Answers for all the Home Practice in the *Discovery Assignment Book* are at the end of the unit.

Lesson 6

Pattern Block Fractions

Lesson Overview

Students use pattern blocks to model fractions. They name fractions when a pattern block is defined as one whole and they identify the whole when a fraction is given. An optional activity, *What's 1?*, is included for students who have not had experiences using pattern blocks to represent fractions.

Key Content

- Representing fractions using pattern blocks.
- Finding a fraction for a given quantity when a unit whole is given.
- Identifying the unit whole when a fraction is given.
- Connecting mathematics to real-life situations.

Key Vocabulary

- hexagon
- rhombus
- trapezoid

Math Facts

DPP Bit M provides practice with math facts. Item P focuses on different aspects of division.

Homework

1. Assign *Questions 1–7* in the Homework section of the *Student Guide*. These questions review skills and concepts addressed in Lessons 1–5.
2. Assign Home Practice Parts 4 and 5.
3. Students continue practicing division facts using the *Triangle Flash Cards: 9s.*

Assessment

Use the *Observational Assessment Record* to note students' abilities to identify the whole when given a fractional part of the whole.

Curriculum Sequence

Before This Unit

Students used pattern blocks to represent fractions and investigate the concept of a whole in Grade 3 Unit 13.

After This Unit

Students will use pattern blocks in Grade 5 to represent fractions in Units 3, 5, and 12. They use them to develop paper-and-pencil procedures for addition, subtraction, and multiplication.

Materials List

Supplies and Copies

Student	Teacher
Supplies for Each Student Pair • 1 set of pattern blocks (2–3 yellow hexagons, 6 red trapezoids, 10 blue rhombuses, 10 green triangles, 6 brown trapezoids)	**Supplies** • overhead pattern blocks, optional
Copies • 1 copy of *What's 1?* per student, optional (*Unit Resource Guide* Pages 88–89)	**Copies/Transparencies**

All blackline masters including assessment, transparency, and DPP masters are also on the Teacher Resource CD.

Student Books

Pattern Block Fractions (*Student Guide* Pages 346–349)

Daily Practice and Problems and Home Practice

DPP items M–P (*Unit Resource Guide* Pages 22–23)
Home Practice Parts 4–5 (*Discovery Assignment Book* Page 195)

Note: Classrooms whose pacing differs significantly from the suggested pacing of the units should use the Math Facts Calendar in Section 4 of the *Facts Resource Guide* to ensure students receive the complete math facts program.

Assessment Tools

Observational Assessment Record (*Unit Resource Guide* Pages 13–14)

M. Bit: Fact Families for × and ÷
(URG p. 22)

Solve the given fact. Then name another fact in the same fact family.

A. $9 \times 8 =$
B. $54 \div 9 =$
C. $36 \div 4 =$
D. $9 \times 7 =$

N. Challenge: Area (URG p. 22)

1. Draw two different shapes on *Centimeter Grid Paper*. Each shape should have an area of 21.5 square centimeters.

2. Measure the perimeter of your two shapes to the nearest tenth of a centimeter. Are the perimeters the same or different?

O. Bit: Evenly Divisible (URG p. 23)

Frank wants to buy stickers for his 6 friends who will be attending his birthday party. At the store, he sees four different collections of stickers.

One pad has 95 stickers.
One pad has 110 stickers.
One pad has 120 stickers.
One pad has 160 stickers.

Frank plans to buy one pad of stickers. If he wants to divide the stickers evenly among his 6 guests without any leftovers, which pad should he purchase? How did you decide?

P. Task: Division Stories (URG p. 23)

Write a division story for $28 \div 9$. Draw a picture for your story and write a number sentence that describes it. In your story, explain any remainder.

In the third grade of the *Math Trailblazers* curriculum, students modeled fractions using pattern blocks. If your students have not experienced using pattern blocks or other manipulatives to represent fractions, have them complete the *What's 1?* Blackline Masters. These pages, taken from the third-grade materials, introduce students to using yellow hexagons, red trapezoids, blue rhombuses, and green triangles to model fractions.

Question 1 asks students to compare sizes and determine the fractional relationships between the various pattern block pieces. These questions are a warm-up for looking at fractional parts of a whole unit.

Questions 2–3 present problems in which students are given the whole and must find the fraction. Some questions also ask students to determine whether the fractions they identify are more than or less than one-half.

Questions 4–5 name a pattern block as a fraction, and students must then determine the unit whole. *Question 6* asks students to make drawings using pattern blocks. For example, *Question 6B* asks students to draw one whole if a green triangle is one-fifth. Note that there are many different shapes that can be drawn with five green triangles.

Questions 7–8 use a six-sided shape (hexagon) that is divided into tenths for one whole. See Figure 16. Ask students to identify the shape by name. Students are to determine both the fraction and decimal fraction for various given parts of the unit whole. For example, because ten greens cover the whole, one green is $\frac{1}{10}$ or 0.1. *Question 7E* asks students to write a fraction for 5 green triangles. Students may name either $\frac{1}{2}$ or $\frac{5}{10}$. Accept both answers and remind students that the two fractions name the same quantity and are equivalent. *Questions 8B–8C* ask students to write two different fractions for one blue rhombus. Since one blue rhombus equals two green triangles, the fractions are $\frac{2}{10}$ and $\frac{1}{5}$. *Question 8D* asks for the decimal fraction for one blue rhombus. Students should realize that $\frac{2}{10}$, $\frac{1}{5}$, and 0.2 all represent the same number.

Part 1 When Are Halves Different?

To begin the activity, students can read the short vignette on the *Pattern Block Fractions* Activity Pages in the *Student Guide*. Jacob and Jerome are discussing their data from the *Bouncing Ball* lab (see Unit 5). They imagine dropping a ball from the top of the Sears Tower in Chicago and from the top of the CN Tower in

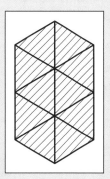

Figure 16: *A hexagon represents 1 whole.*

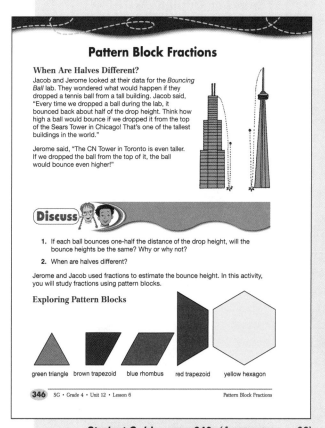

Student Guide - page 346 (Answers on p. 90)

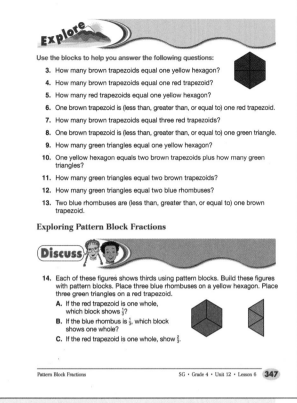

Student Guide - page 347 (Answers on p. 90)

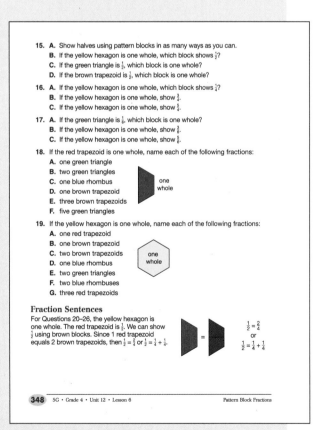

Student Guide - page 348 (Answers on p. 91)

Toronto. **Question 1** asks if each ball bounces $\frac{1}{2}$ the distance of the drop height, will they both bounce to the same height? Students will see that the bounce height for each ball will be different, but it may be more difficult for them to explain why. If the drop heights are different, halves of the drop heights will also be different. Halves are different when the unit wholes are different (**Question 2**). The size of a fraction depends on the size of the whole. Working on the questions in this lesson will help students understand this concept.

Part 2 Exploring Pattern Blocks

As mentioned, in third grade, students used pattern blocks in studying fractions. They used the yellow hexagons, red trapezoids, blue rhombuses, and green triangles. When the yellow hexagon is designated as the whole, students can work with halves, thirds, and sixths using these blocks. In this lesson, students add brown trapezoids. The brown trapezoid is one-fourth of the yellow hexagon. **Questions 3–13** guide students through an exploration of the relative sizes of the five kinds of pattern blocks. Figure 17 shows the brown trapezoid in relation to a yellow hexagon.

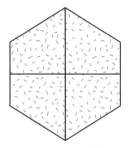

Figure 17: *A brown trapezoid is $\frac{1}{4}$ of the yellow hexagon.*

Part 3 Exploring Pattern Block Fractions

Questions 14–19 ask students to name fractions when the whole is given and name the whole when a fraction is given. For example, **Question 14** asks students to show thirds in different ways using pattern blocks. See Figure 18. They identify the green triangle as $\frac{1}{3}$ of a red trapezoid and identify the yellow hexagon as one whole when the blue rhombus is $\frac{1}{3}$.

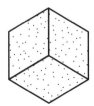

Figure 18: *Showing thirds using pattern blocks*

Question 18 asks students to name the fractions that different pattern blocks represent if the red trapezoid is one whole. **Question 19** asks them to do the same when the yellow hexagon is one whole. Answering these questions will help students solve the puzzles posed in Lesson 8 *Fraction Puzzles.* Note that **Question 18F** asks for the fraction name for five green triangles if the red trapezoid is one whole. See Figure 19. Students can give either the improper fraction ($\frac{5}{3}$) or the mixed number $1\frac{2}{3}$. Point out to students that both answers are correct and represent the same quantity.

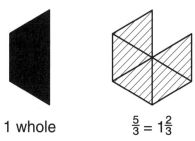

1 whole $\frac{5}{3} = 1\frac{2}{3}$

Figure 19: *If the red trapezoid is one whole, five green triangles are $\frac{5}{3}$ or $1\frac{2}{3}$.*

Part 4 Fraction Sentences

Questions 20–26 ask students to model easy addition problems using pattern blocks. Although they do not learn pencil-and-paper procedures for adding unlike fractions until fifth grade, using manipulatives provides students with a strategy for adding unlike fractions without finding common denominators. For example, **Question 23** asks them to show $\frac{1}{2}$ using two or more colors and then to write a number sentence for their results. Figure 20 shows a red trapezoid ($\frac{1}{2}$) covered by a green triangle ($\frac{1}{6}$) and a blue rhombus ($\frac{1}{3}$). Students write $\frac{1}{2} = \frac{1}{6} + \frac{1}{3}$ to represent this figure.

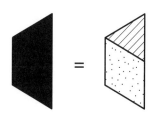

Figure 20: $\frac{1}{2} = \frac{1}{6} + \frac{1}{3}$

20. Show $\frac{1}{2}$ using green blocks. (Cover a red trapezoid with green blocks.) Write a number sentence to represent this figure.

21. The blue rhombus is $\frac{1}{3}$. Show $\frac{1}{3}$ using green blocks, and write a number sentence to represent this figure.

We can show 1 whole with two or more colors and write a number sentence to represent the figure.

22. Show 1 whole another way using two or more colors. Write a number sentence for your figure.

$1 = \frac{2}{4} + \frac{1}{6} + \frac{1}{3}$

For Questions 23–26, show each fraction using two or more colors. Write a number sentence for each figure.

23. Show $\frac{1}{2}$.   24. Show $\frac{3}{4}$.

25. Show $\frac{2}{3}$.   26. Show $\frac{3}{2}$.

Homework

Use your fraction chart from Lesson 3 or imagine pattern blocks to help you solve these problems.

1. Michael used $\frac{1}{2}$ yard of ribbon to decorate a gift for his mother. Irma used $\frac{2}{3}$ yard for her mother's present. Who used more ribbon?

2. Lee Yah drank $\frac{1}{3}$ cup of juice, and Roberto drank $\frac{1}{2}$ cup. Who drank more juice?

3. Put these fractions in order from smallest to largest: $\frac{5}{8}, \frac{1}{4}, \frac{1}{2}$.

4. Put these fractions in order from smallest to largest: $\frac{1}{2}, \frac{1}{3}, \frac{3}{4}$.

5. Put these fractions in order from smallest to largest: $\frac{2}{3}, \frac{1}{2}, \frac{1}{6}$. Explain your strategy.

6. Add or subtract.

   A. $\frac{2}{6} + \frac{3}{6} =$ B. $\frac{1}{4} + \frac{2}{4} =$

   C. $\frac{1}{3} + \frac{2}{3} =$ D. $\frac{3}{4} - \frac{1}{4} =$

   E. $\frac{5}{6} - \frac{2}{6} =$ F. $\frac{3}{3} - \frac{1}{3} =$

7. Write three equivalent fractions for $\frac{3}{4}$.

Student Guide - page 349 (Answers on p. 92)

DPP Bit M provides practice with the division facts for the nines through the use of fact families. Task P asks students to write a story for a division problem.

Homework and Practice

- The Homework section in the *Student Guide* reviews skills and concepts developed in the first five lessons of this unit.
- DPP Bit O poses a divisibility question and asks students to explain their strategies.
- Remind students to practice the division facts for the nines using their *Triangle Flash Cards.*
- Assign Home Practice Parts 4 and 5. Students will need their fraction charts and a meterstick for Part 5.

Answers for Parts 4 and 5 of the Home Practice are in the Answer Key at the end of this lesson and at the end of this unit.

Assessment

- Use the *Observational Assessment Record* to note students' abilities to identify the whole when given a fractional part of the whole.
- Check students' homework to assess their abilities to compare fractions, add and subtract fractions with like denominators, and find equivalent fractions.

Extension

DPP Challenge N provides an open-response problem concerning area and perimeter.

Name _____ Date _____

PART 4 Fractions and Decimals
Complete this table. The flat equals one whole.

Base-Ten Shorthand	Common Fraction	Decimal Fraction
|/	$\frac{25}{100}$ or $\frac{1}{4}$	0.25
□·		
		0.03
□□□□□ /|/||		
	$\frac{3}{10}$	
		4.37
□□		
	$4\frac{16}{100}$	
		10.41

PART 5 A Fraction of a Meter
Use your fraction chart from Lesson 3, the Fraction Chart in your *Student Guide,* or a meterstick to help you compare fractions.

1. Name a measurement that is greater than $\frac{1}{2}$ meter but less than $\frac{7}{10}$ of a meter.
2. Which is longer: $\frac{7}{10}$ of a meter or 50 centimeters?
3. Name a measurement that is a little less than $\frac{3}{10}$ of a meter.
4. Name a fraction of a meter that is longer than $\frac{3}{100}$ of a meter and shorter than 0.2 meter.
5. Name a fraction that is less than $\frac{7}{10}$ but more than $\frac{1}{5}$.
6. Name a measurement that is longer than 1.54 meters but shorter than $1\frac{9}{10}$ meters.
7. Name a measurement that is more than three times as long as $\frac{1}{2}$ of a meter.

EXPLORING FRACTIONS   DAB • Grade 4 • Unit 12 **195**

Discovery Assignment Book - page 195 (Answers on p. 93)

At a Glance

Math Facts and Daily Practice and Problems

DPP Bit M provides practice with math facts. Items O and P focus on different aspects of division. Challenge N provides a problem involving area and perimeter.

Before the Activity

If students are new to the curriculum or if they have not experienced using pattern blocks to represent fractions, have them complete a third-grade activity found in the Unit Resource Guide, *What's 1?*, to introduce pattern block fractions.

Part 1. When Are Halves Different?

1. Students read the first section on the *Pattern Block Fractions* Activity Pages in the *Student Guide*.
2. Discuss *Questions 1–2*.

Part 2. Exploring Pattern Blocks

1. Distribute one set of pattern blocks to each pair of students.
2. Students explore pattern block fractions by completing *Questions 3–13* in the *Student Guide*.

Part 3. Exploring Pattern Block Fractions

Students identify wholes from given fractions using pattern blocks in *Questions 14–19*.

Part 4. Fraction Sentences

Students model easy addition and subtraction problems using pattern blocks in *Questions 20–26*.

Homework

1. Assign *Questions 1–7* in the Homework section of the *Student Guide*. These questions review skills and concepts addressed in Lessons 1–5.
2. Assign Home Practice Parts 4 and 5.
3. Students continue practicing division facts using the *Triangle Flash Cards: 9s*.

Assessment

Use the *Observational Assessment Record* to note students' abilities to identify the whole when given a fractional part of the whole.

Extension

Use DPP item N to challenge students with an open-response problem.

Answer Key is on pages 90–95.

Notes:

What's 1?

Use yellow hexagons, red trapezoids, blue rhombuses, and green triangles to answer the following questions.

Covering Pattern Blocks

1. Look at all your pieces to answer these questions.

   A. How many red trapezoids cover one yellow hexagon?

   B. How many blue rhombuses cover one yellow hexagon?

   C. How many green triangles cover one yellow hexagon?

   D. How many green triangles cover one blue rhombus?

   E. How many green triangles cover one red trapezoid?

   F. Use two different colors to cover one red trapezoid. What did you use?

Wholes to Parts

2. If the yellow hexagon is one whole, then:

   A. What piece is one-half?

   B. What piece is one-third?

   C. What piece is one-sixth?

   D. We can write $\frac{2}{6}$ for 2 green triangles. Write a number for 5 green triangles.

   E. Write a number for 2 blue rhombuses.

   F. Write a number for 3 red trapezoids.

   G. Write a number for 4 red trapezoids.

   H. Is 1 blue rhombus more or less than one-half?

   I. Are 2 blue rhombuses more or less than one-half?

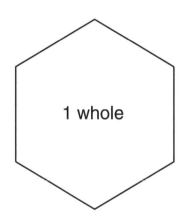

1 whole

3. This shape is one whole.

   A. How many blue rhombuses cover the shape?

   B. How many green triangles cover the shape?

   C. What piece is one-half?

   D. What piece is one-fourth?

   E. Write a fraction for 3 green triangles.

   F. What other piece makes the same fraction as 3 green triangles?

   G. Is 1 red trapezoid more or less than one-half?

1 whole

Parts to Wholes

4. If the green triangle is one-half, what piece is one whole?

5. If the blue rhombus is one-third, what is one whole?

6. Trace pattern blocks on a sheet of paper to answer these questions. For example, if the green triangle is $\frac{1}{3}$, draw one whole.

 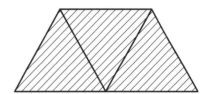

A. If the green triangle is $\frac{1}{3}$, draw $\frac{2}{3}$.

B. If the green triangle is $\frac{1}{5}$, draw one whole.

C. If the red trapezoid is $\frac{1}{3}$, draw one whole.

D. If the yellow hexagon is $\frac{1}{2}$, draw one whole.

E. If the blue rhombus is $\frac{1}{4}$, draw $\frac{3}{4}$.

7. The shape to the right is one whole.

   A. How many green triangles cover the shape?

   B. Write a common fraction for 1 green triangle.

   C. Write a decimal for 1 green triangle.

   D. Write a fraction and a decimal for 7 green triangles.

   E. Write a fraction and a decimal for 5 green triangles.

8. The shape to the right is one whole.

   A. How many blue rhombuses cover the whole?

   B. Write a common fraction for 1 blue rhombus.

   C. Write a different fraction for 1 blue rhombus.

   D. Write a decimal for 1 blue rhombus.

   E. Write a fraction for 1 yellow hexagon.

   F. Is 1 yellow hexagon more or less than one-half?

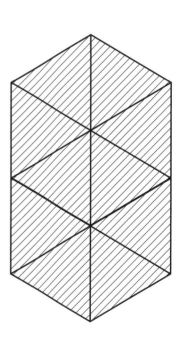

9. A. If the blue rhombus is one whole, write a number for 3 green triangles.

   B. If the blue rhombus is one whole, write a number for 1 yellow hexagon.

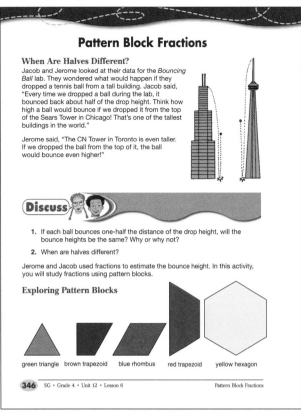

Student Guide - page 346

Student Guide (p. 346)

Pattern Block Fractions

1. No, because the drop heights for each one are different.*

2. When the wholes are different in size.*

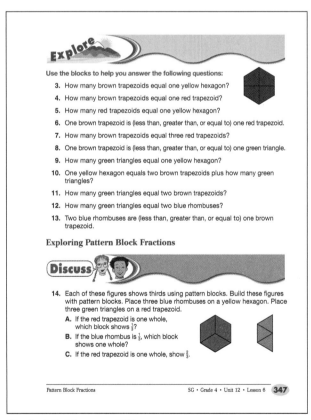

Student Guide - page 347

Student Guide (p. 347)

3. 4*

4. 2

5. 2

6. less than

7. 6

8. greater than

9. 6

10. 3

11. 3

12. 4

13. greater than

14. **A.** green triangle*

    B. yellow hexagon*

    C.

*Answers and/or discussion are included in the Lesson Guide.

Student Guide (p. 348)

15. A.

B. red trapezoid

C. blue rhombus

D. red trapezoid

16. A. brown trapezoid

B.

C.

17. A. yellow hexagon

B.

C.

18. A. $\frac{1}{3}$*

B. $\frac{2}{3}$

C. $\frac{2}{3}$

D. $\frac{1}{2}$

E. $1\frac{1}{2}$ or $\frac{3}{2}$

F. $1\frac{2}{3}$ or $\frac{5}{3}$*

19. A. $\frac{1}{2}$*

B. $\frac{1}{4}$

C. $\frac{2}{4}$

D. $\frac{1}{3}$

E. $\frac{2}{6}$

F. $\frac{2}{3}$

G. $\frac{3}{2}$ or $1\frac{1}{2}$

---

15. A. Show halves using pattern blocks in as many ways as you can.
  B. If the yellow hexagon is one whole, which block shows $\frac{1}{2}$?
  C. If the green triangle is $\frac{1}{2}$, which block is one whole?
  D. If the brown trapezoid is $\frac{1}{2}$, which block is one whole?

16. A. If the yellow hexagon is one whole, which block shows $\frac{1}{4}$?
  B. If the yellow hexagon is one whole, show $\frac{3}{4}$.
  C. If the yellow hexagon is one whole, show $\frac{5}{4}$.

17. A. If the green triangle is $\frac{1}{6}$, which block is one whole?
  B. If the yellow hexagon is one whole, show $\frac{3}{6}$.
  C. If the yellow hexagon is one whole, show $\frac{6}{6}$.

18. If the red trapezoid is one whole, name each of the following fractions:
  A. one green triangle
  B. two green triangles
  C. one blue rhombus
  D. one brown trapezoid
  E. three brown trapezoids
  F. five green triangles

 one whole

19. If the yellow hexagon is one whole, name each of the following fractions:
  A. one red trapezoid
  B. one brown trapezoid
  C. two brown trapezoids
  D. one blue rhombus
  E. two green triangles
  F. two blue rhombuses
  G. three red trapezoids

one whole

Fraction Sentences

For Questions 20–26, the yellow hexagon is one whole. The red trapezoid is $\frac{1}{2}$. We can show $\frac{1}{2}$ using brown blocks. Since 1 red trapezoid equals 2 brown trapezoids, then $\frac{1}{2} = \frac{2}{4}$ or $\frac{1}{2} = \frac{1}{4} + \frac{1}{4}$.

= $\frac{1}{2} = \frac{2}{4}$
or
$\frac{1}{2} = \frac{1}{4} + \frac{1}{4}$

Student Guide - page 348

---

*Answers and/or discussion are included in the Lesson Guide.

20. Show $\frac{1}{2}$ using green blocks. (Cover a red trapezoid with green blocks.) Write a number sentence to represent this figure.

21. The blue rhombus is $\frac{1}{3}$. Show $\frac{1}{3}$ using green blocks, and write a number sentence to represent this figure.

We can show 1 whole with two or more colors and write a number sentence to represent the figure.

$1 = \frac{2}{4} + \frac{1}{6} + \frac{1}{3}$

22. Show 1 whole another way using two or more colors. Write a number sentence for your figure.

For Questions 23–26, show each fraction using two or more colors. Write a number sentence for each figure.

23. Show $\frac{1}{2}$. 24. Show $\frac{3}{4}$.

25. Show $\frac{2}{3}$. 26. Show $\frac{3}{2}$.

Homework

Use your fraction chart from Lesson 3 or imagine pattern blocks to help you solve these problems.

1. Michael used $\frac{1}{2}$ yard of ribbon to decorate a gift for his mother. Irma used $\frac{2}{3}$ yard for her mother's present. Who used more ribbon?

2. Lee Yah drank $\frac{1}{3}$ cup of juice, and Roberto drank $\frac{1}{2}$ cup. Who drank more juice?

3. Put these fractions in order from smallest to largest: $\frac{5}{6}, \frac{1}{4}, \frac{1}{2}$.

4. Put these fractions in order from smallest to largest: $\frac{1}{2}, \frac{1}{3}, \frac{3}{4}$.

5. Put these fractions in order from smallest to largest: $\frac{2}{3}, \frac{1}{2}, \frac{1}{6}$. Explain your strategy.

6. Add or subtract.
   A. $\frac{2}{6} + \frac{3}{6} =$ B. $\frac{1}{4} + \frac{2}{4} =$
   C. $\frac{1}{3} + \frac{2}{3} =$ D. $\frac{3}{4} - \frac{1}{4} =$
   E. $\frac{5}{6} - \frac{2}{6} =$ F. $\frac{3}{3} - \frac{1}{3} =$

7. Write three equivalent fractions for $\frac{3}{4}$.

Pattern Block Fractions   SG • Grade 4 • Unit 12 • Lesson 6   **349**

Student Guide - page 349

Student Guide (p. 349)

20. $\frac{3}{6} = \frac{1}{2}$ or $\frac{1}{6} + \frac{1}{6} + \frac{1}{6} = \frac{1}{2}$

21. $\frac{1}{3} = \frac{2}{6}$ or $\frac{1}{6} + \frac{1}{6} = \frac{1}{3}$ $=$

22. Answers will vary.

23. $\frac{1}{3} + \frac{1}{6} = \frac{1}{2}$*

24. Answers will vary. Two possible answers:

    $\frac{1}{2} + \frac{1}{4} = \frac{3}{4}$

    $\frac{3}{6} + \frac{1}{4} = \frac{3}{4}$

25. $\frac{2}{6} + \frac{1}{3} = \frac{2}{3}$

26. Answers will vary. Two possible answers:

    $\frac{1}{2} + \frac{1}{6} + \frac{1}{3} + \frac{2}{4} = \frac{3}{2}$

    $\frac{1}{2} + \frac{4}{4} = \frac{3}{2}$

Homework

1. Irma   2. Roberto

3. $\frac{1}{4}, \frac{1}{2}, \frac{5}{6}$ 4. $\frac{1}{3}, \frac{1}{2}, \frac{3}{4}$

5. $\frac{1}{6}, \frac{1}{2}, \frac{2}{3}$. Possible strategies include using the fraction chart or using $\frac{1}{2}$ as a benchmark. $\frac{1}{6}$ is less than $\frac{1}{2}$ and $\frac{2}{3}$ is more than $\frac{1}{2}$.

6. A. $\frac{5}{6}$ B. $\frac{3}{4}$
   C. $\frac{3}{3}$ or 1   D. $\frac{2}{4}$
   E. $\frac{3}{6}$ F. $\frac{2}{3}$

7. Answers will vary.

*Answers and/or discussion are included in the Lesson Guide.

Discovery Assignment Book (p. 195)

Home Practice*

Part 4. Fractions and Decimals

Base-Ten Shorthand	Common Fraction	Decimal Fraction
|/ ·\·\··	$\frac{25}{100}$ or $\frac{1}{4}$	0.25
☐·	$1\frac{1}{100}$	1.01
·\··	$\frac{3}{100}$	0.03
☐☐☐☐☐ /\/\\	$5\frac{5}{10}$ or $5\frac{1}{2}$	5.5
/|	$\frac{3}{10}$	0.3
☐☐☐☐/\\··\···	$4\frac{37}{100}$	4.37
☐☐·\··	$2\frac{4}{100}$	2.04
☐☐☐☐/·\··	$4\frac{16}{100}$	4.16
☐|/\\\|·	$10\frac{41}{100}$	10.41

Part 5. A Fraction of a Meter

1. Answers will vary. Possible response: $\frac{6}{10}$ m

2. $\frac{7}{10}$ of a meter

3. Answers will vary. Possible responses: 25 cm or 0.25 m

4. Answers will vary. Possible response: $\frac{1}{10}$ m

5. Answers will vary. Possible response: $\frac{1}{2}$

6. Answers will vary. Possible responses: $1\frac{3}{4}$ or 1.75 meters

7. Answers will vary. Possible response: 2 meters

Name _____ Date _____

PART 4 Fractions and Decimals
Complete this table. The flat equals one whole.

Base-Ten Shorthand	Common Fraction	Decimal Fraction
|/ ·····	$\frac{25}{100}$ or $\frac{1}{4}$	0.25
☐·		
		0.03
☐☐☐☐☐ /\/\\		
	$\frac{3}{10}$	
		4.37
☐☐ ····		
	$4\frac{16}{100}$	
		10.41

PART 5 A Fraction of a Meter
Use your fraction chart from Lesson 3, the Fraction Chart in your *Student Guide*, or a meterstick to help you compare fractions.

1. Name a measurement that is greater than $\frac{1}{2}$ meter but less than $\frac{7}{10}$ of a meter.
2. Which is longer: $\frac{7}{10}$ of a meter or 50 centimeters?
3. Name a measurement that is a little less than $\frac{3}{10}$ of a meter.
4. Name a fraction of a meter that is longer than $\frac{5}{100}$ of a meter and shorter than 0.2 meter.
5. Name a fraction that is less than $\frac{7}{10}$ but more than $\frac{1}{6}$.
6. Name a measurement that is longer than 1.54 meters but shorter than $1\frac{9}{10}$ meters.
7. Name a measurement that is more than three times as long as $\frac{1}{2}$ of a meter.

EXPLORING FRACTIONS   DAB • Grade 4 • Unit 12 **195**

Discovery Assignment Book - page 195

---

*Answers for all the Home Practice in the *Discovery Assignment Book* are at the end of the unit.

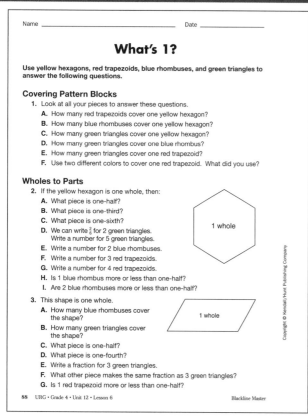

Unit Resource Guide - page 88

Unit Resource Guide (p. 88)

What's 1?

I. A. 2

   B. 3

   C. 6

   D. 2

   E. 3

   F. 1 blue rhombus and 1 green triangle

2. A. red trapezoid

   B. blue rhombus

   C. green triangle

   D. $\frac{5}{6}$

   E. $\frac{2}{3}$

   F. $1\frac{1}{2}$ or $\frac{3}{2}$

   G. $\frac{4}{2}$ or 2

   H. less

   I. more

3. A. 2

   B. 4

   C. blue rhombus

   D. green triangle

   E. $\frac{3}{4}$

   F. red trapezoid

   G. more

*Answers and/or discussion are included in the Lesson Guide.

Unit Resource Guide (p. 89)

4. blue rhombus

5. yellow hexagon

6. A.

   B.*

   C.

   D.

   E.

7. A. 10*

   B. $\frac{1}{10}$*

   C. 0.1*

   D. $\frac{7}{10}$ and 0.7

   E. $\frac{5}{10}$ or $\frac{1}{2}$ and 0.5*

8. A. 5

   B. $\frac{2}{10}$ or $\frac{1}{5}$*

   C. $\frac{1}{5}$ or $\frac{2}{10}$*

   D. 0.2*

   E. $\frac{6}{10}$ or $\frac{3}{5}$

   F. more

9. A. $\frac{3}{2}$ or $1\frac{1}{2}$

   B. 3

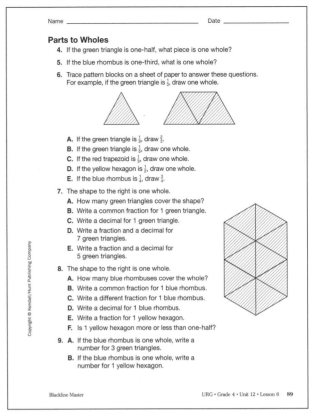

Name _____ Date _____

Parts to Wholes

4. If the green triangle is one-half, what piece is one whole?

5. If the blue rhombus is one-third, what is one whole?

6. Trace pattern blocks on a sheet of paper to answer these questions. For example, if the green triangle is $\frac{1}{3}$, draw one whole.

   A. If the green triangle is $\frac{1}{3}$, draw $\frac{2}{3}$.
   B. If the green triangle is $\frac{1}{6}$, draw one whole.
   C. If the red trapezoid is $\frac{1}{3}$, draw one whole.
   D. If the yellow hexagon is $\frac{1}{2}$, draw one whole.
   E. If the blue rhombus is $\frac{1}{4}$, draw $\frac{3}{4}$.

7. The shape to the right is one whole.
   A. How many green triangles cover the shape?
   B. Write a common fraction for 1 green triangle.
   C. Write a decimal for 1 green triangle.
   D. Write a fraction and a decimal for 7 green triangles.
   E. Write a fraction and a decimal for 5 green triangles.

8. The shape to the right is one whole.
   A. How many blue rhombuses cover the whole?
   B. Write a common fraction for 1 blue rhombus.
   C. Write a different fraction for 1 blue rhombus.
   D. Write a decimal for 1 blue rhombus.
   E. Write a fraction for 1 yellow hexagon.
   F. Is 1 yellow hexagon more or less than one-half?

9. A. If the blue rhombus is one whole, write a number for 3 green triangles.
   B. If the blue rhombus is one whole, write a number for 1 yellow hexagon.

Blackline Master   URG • Grade 4 • Unit 12 • Lesson 6   89

Unit Resource Guide - page 89

*Answers and/or discussion are included in the Lesson Guide.

Lesson 7

Solving Problems with Pattern Blocks

Lesson Overview

Estimated Class Sessions

1

Students use pattern blocks to solve word problems involving the ordering of fractions. Using the context of dividing food fairly, they investigate the relationship between the number of equal parts in the whole (the size of the denominator) and the size of the fraction. For example, they can reason that $\frac{1}{3}$ is greater than $\frac{1}{4}$ because if you divide a pizza into four parts, the parts will be smaller than if you divide the pizza into three parts. Students also use pattern blocks to solve word problems involving addition of fractions.

Key Content

- Solving multistep word problems.
- Comparing and ordering fractions.
- Adding fractions using manipulatives.
- Connecting mathematics to real-world situations.

Homework

Assign *Questions 1–5* in the Homework section in the *Student Guide*.

Assessment

Use DPP items Q and R as assessments.

Materials List

Supplies and Copies

Student	Teacher
Supplies for Each Student Pair • 1 set of pattern blocks (2–3 yellow hexagons, 6 red trapezoids, 10 blue rhombuses, 10 green triangles, 6 brown trapezoids) • 1 fraction chart from Lesson 3	**Supplies** • overhead pattern blocks, optional
Copies	**Copies/Transparencies**

All blackline masters including assessment, transparency, and DPP masters are also on the Teacher Resource CD.

Student Books

Fraction Chart from *Comparing Fractions* (*Student Guide* Page 336)
Solving Problems with Pattern Blocks (*Student Guide* Pages 350–352)

Daily Practice and Problems and Home Practice

DPP items Q–R (*Unit Resource Guide* Pages 23–24)

Note: Classrooms whose pacing differs significantly from the suggested pacing of the units should use the Math Facts Calendar in Section 4 of the *Facts Resource Guide* to ensure students receive the complete math facts program.

Q. Bit: Confused! (URG p. 23)

On planet Zimbo, a Zimbonese was told that the number 6 is larger than the number 4. But now there is confusion because the Zimbonese was also told that $\frac{1}{6}$ is smaller than $\frac{1}{4}$. Please use a diagram to explain why $\frac{1}{6}$ is smaller than $\frac{1}{4}$.

R. Task: Further Confusion (URG p. 24)

Brandon and Lee Yah invited the Zimbonese to eat pizza with them. Brandon has $\frac{1}{8}$ of a pizza and it is bigger in size than Lee Yah's $\frac{1}{4}$ of a pizza. The Zimbonese thought it understood (see DPP Bit Q) that $\frac{1}{8}$ was smaller than $\frac{1}{4}$. What needs to be changed so that $\frac{1}{8}$ is less than $\frac{1}{4}$?

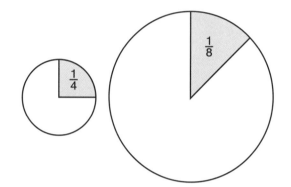

Students can work in pairs to complete *Questions 1–8* on the *Solving Problems with Pattern Blocks* Activity Pages in the *Student Guide.* Then, the student pairs can report their strategies and solutions to the class.

Questions 1–3 ask students to name fractions when the whole is divided into different numbers of equal parts and then to compare the fractions. For example, to answer *Question 2,* students find that John ate $\frac{2}{12}$ of a pie, Shannon ate $\frac{2}{6}$ of a pie, and Brandon ate $\frac{2}{4}$ of a pie. They must then decide who ate the most and the least amount of pie. Students can reason that when the pies are divided into more pieces, the pieces will be smaller. *Question 3* is a whimsical version of the same problem using nonsense words. Students may use their fraction chart from Lesson 3 to help them think through the problem. If one whole is divided into eight zax and the same size whole is divided into ten snarks, what fraction is one zax? What fraction is one snark? Which fraction is larger? One zax is $\frac{1}{8}$ of the whole and one snark is $\frac{1}{10}$. One-eighth is larger since the whole has been divided into fewer pieces.

Question 4 asks students to order fractions that have like numerators and unlike denominators. They solved similar problems using the Fraction Chart in Lesson 3. *Questions 4A–4B* can also be modeled using pattern blocks. *Questions 4C–4D* can be solved using the Fraction Chart or using the reasoning they developed answering *Questions 1–3.*

Question 5 asks students to describe a strategy for ordering fractions if the numerators are the same. One possible response: "When the numerators are the same, the smaller the denominator, the larger the fraction because the whole is divided into fewer parts."

Questions 6–8 are word problems which involve adding fractions. Some of the problems in *Question 6* involve adding fractions with unlike denominators, so they will need to use tools such as pattern blocks (as they did in Lesson 6) or drawings to solve the problems. By solving problems using manipulatives, students build a conceptual foundation for pencil and paper procedures and they develop number sense with fractions. *Questions 7–8* are problems that can be solved using repeated addition. Students may choose to write an addition number sentence or a multiplication number sentence. For example, *Question 7A* asks how many muffins are eaten if four students each eat $\frac{1}{2}$ of a muffin. After modeling the problem with pattern blocks, students may write $\frac{1}{2} + \frac{1}{2} + \frac{1}{2} + \frac{1}{2} = 2$ muffins or $4 \times \frac{1}{2} = 2$ muffins.

Solving Problems with Pattern Blocks

You may use pattern blocks or your fraction chart to help you solve these problems.

1. Wednesday is pizza day at Bessie Coleman School. Each table in the lunchroom gets one pizza to share fairly among the students at the table. There are three students at Table A and four students at Table B.
   A. What fraction of the pizza will each student at Table A get?
   B. What fraction of the pizza will each student at Table B get?
   C. Who gets to eat more pizza, the students at Table A or the students at Table B?
   D. Which fraction is larger, $\frac{1}{3}$ or $\frac{1}{4}$? Explain how you know.

2. The cook made three small fruit pies that are all the same size. She divided the apple pie into 12 pieces, the cherry pie into six pieces, and the peach pie into four pieces. John ate two pieces of apple pie, Shannon ate two pieces of cherry pie, and Brandon ate two pieces of peach pie.

   A. What fraction of the apple pie did John eat?
   B. What fraction of the cherry pie did Shannon eat?
   C. What fraction of the peach pie did Brandon eat?
   D. Who ate the most pie? Tell how you know.
   E. Who ate the least pie?

3. One whole is divided into eight zax. Each zax is the same size. The same size whole is divided into ten snarks. Each snark is the same size.
   A. What fraction of the whole is one zax?
   B. What fraction of the whole is one snark?
   C. Which is larger, one zax or one snark? Explain.

Student Guide - page 350 (Answers on p. 102)

4. Put each group of fractions in order from smallest to largest.
   A. $\frac{1}{2}, \frac{1}{6}, \frac{1}{3}, \frac{1}{4}, \frac{1}{12}$
   B. $\frac{2}{6}, \frac{2}{3}, \frac{2}{4}, \frac{2}{12}$
   C. $\frac{1}{10}, \frac{1}{8}, \frac{1}{5}$
   D. $\frac{3}{10}, \frac{3}{8}, \frac{3}{5}$

5. Describe a strategy for ordering fractions if the numerators are the same.

To solve the problems in Questions 6–8, you may use any tools such as pattern blocks, the Fraction Chart in Lesson 3, or pictures. Write number sentences to record your solutions.

6. Each of the following pairs of students shared a pizza. How much of the whole pizza did each pair eat?
   A. Manny ate $\frac{1}{2}$ of a pizza and Ming ate $\frac{1}{4}$ of it.
   B. Michael ate $\frac{3}{8}$ of a pizza and Frank ate $\frac{5}{8}$.
   C. Felicia ate $\frac{1}{3}$ of a pizza. Linda ate $\frac{1}{6}$ of it.
   D. Lee Yah ate $\frac{5}{12}$ and David ate $\frac{2}{12}$.

7. A. Four students each ate $\frac{1}{2}$ of a muffin. How many muffins did they eat altogether?
   B. Five students each ate $\frac{1}{2}$ of a muffin. How many muffins did they eat altogether?

8. A. Eight students each ate $\frac{1}{4}$ of an apple. How many apples did they eat altogether?
   B. Three students each ate $\frac{1}{4}$ of an apple. How many apples did they eat altogether?
   C. Six students each ate $\frac{1}{4}$ of an apple. How many apples did they eat altogether?

Student Guide - page 351 (Answers on p. 102)

Journal Prompt

One whole is divided equally into 100 widgets. The same size whole is divided into 50 zittles. What fraction of a whole is one widget? What fraction of a whole is one zittle? Which is larger, a widget or a zittle? Explain.

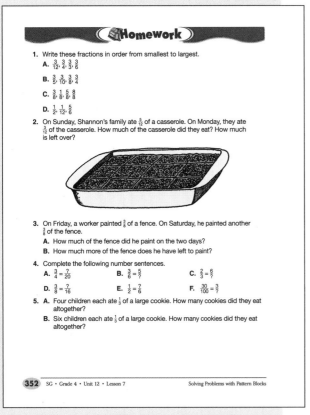

Homework

1. Write these fractions in order from smallest to largest.
   A. $\frac{3}{12}, \frac{3}{4}, \frac{3}{3}, \frac{3}{6}$

   B. $\frac{3}{5}, \frac{3}{10}, \frac{3}{8}, \frac{3}{4}$

   C. $\frac{3}{8}, \frac{1}{8}, \frac{5}{8}, \frac{8}{8}$

   D. $\frac{1}{2}, \frac{1}{12}, \frac{5}{6}$

2. On Sunday, Shannon's family ate $\frac{5}{12}$ of a casserole. On Monday, they ate $\frac{3}{12}$ of the casserole. How much of the casserole did they eat? How much is left over?

3. On Friday, a worker painted $\frac{3}{8}$ of a fence. On Saturday, he painted another $\frac{3}{8}$ of the fence.
   A. How much of the fence did he paint on the two days?
   B. How much more of the fence does he have left to paint?

4. Complete the following number sentences.
   A. $\frac{3}{4} = \frac{?}{20}$ B. $\frac{3}{6} = \frac{5}{?}$ C. $\frac{2}{3} = \frac{6}{?}$

   D. $\frac{3}{8} = \frac{?}{16}$ E. $\frac{1}{2} = \frac{?}{6}$ F. $\frac{30}{100} = \frac{3}{?}$

5. A. Four children each ate $\frac{1}{3}$ of a large cookie. How many cookies did they eat altogether?
   B. Six children each ate $\frac{1}{3}$ of a large cookie. How many cookies did they eat altogether?

352   SG • Grade 4 • Unit 12 • Lesson 7   Solving Problems with Pattern Blocks

Student Guide - page 352   *(Answers on p. 103)*

Homework and Practice

Questions 1–5 in the Homework section of the *Student Guide* provide practice ordering fractions, finding equivalent fractions, and adding fractions with like denominators.

Assessment

Use DPP items Q and R to assess students' understanding of fraction concepts.

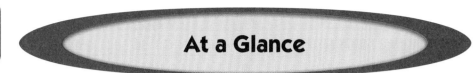
Math Facts and Daily Practice and Problems

DPP items Q and R review basic fraction concepts.

Teaching the Activity

1. Students solve problems on the *Solving Problems with Pattern Blocks* Activity Pages in the *Student Guide.* They order fractions and develop strategies for comparing fractions with like numerators *(Questions 1–5).*

2. Students solve problems involving addition of fractions using manipulatives or drawings *(Questions 6–8).*

Homework

Assign *Questions 1–5* in the Homework section in the *Student Guide.*

Assessment

Use DPP items Q and R as assessments.

Answer Key is on pages 102–103.

Notes:

Solving Problems with Pattern Blocks

You may use pattern blocks or your fraction chart to help you solve these problems.

1. Wednesday is pizza day at Bessie Coleman School. Each table in the lunchroom gets one pizza to share fairly among the students at the table. There are three students at Table A and four students at Table B.
   A. What fraction of the pizza will each student at Table A get?
   B. What fraction of the pizza will each student at Table B get?
   C. Who gets to eat more pizza, the students at Table A or the students at Table B?
   D. Which fraction is larger, $\frac{1}{3}$ or $\frac{1}{4}$? Explain how you know.

2. The cook made three small fruit pies that are all the same size. She divided the apple pie into 12 pieces, the cherry pie into six pieces, and the peach pie into four pieces. John ate two pieces of apple pie, Shannon ate two pieces of cherry pie, and Brandon ate two pieces of peach pie.

   A. What fraction of the apple pie did John eat?
   B. What fraction of the cherry pie did Shannon eat?
   C. What fraction of the peach pie did Brandon eat?
   D. Who ate the most pie? Tell how you know.
   E. Who ate the least pie?

3. One whole is divided into eight zax. Each zax is the same size. The same size whole is divided into ten snarks. Each snark is the same size.
   A. What fraction of the whole is one zax?
   B. What fraction of the whole is one snark?
   C. Which is larger, one zax or one snark? Explain.

Student Guide - page 350

4. Put each group of fractions in order from smallest to largest.
   A. $\frac{1}{2}, \frac{1}{6}, \frac{1}{3}, \frac{1}{4}, \frac{1}{12}$
   B. $\frac{2}{6}, \frac{2}{3}, \frac{2}{4}, \frac{2}{12}$
   C. $\frac{1}{10}, \frac{1}{8}, \frac{1}{5}$
   D. $\frac{3}{10}, \frac{3}{8}, \frac{3}{5}$

5. Describe a strategy for ordering fractions if the numerators are the same.

To solve the problems in Questions 6–8, you may use any tools such as pattern blocks, the Fraction Chart in Lesson 3, or pictures. Write number sentences to record your solutions.

6. Each of the following pairs of students shared a pizza. How much of the whole pizza did each pair eat?
   A. Manny ate $\frac{1}{2}$ of a pizza and Ming ate $\frac{1}{4}$ of it.
   B. Michael ate $\frac{3}{8}$ of a pizza and Frank ate $\frac{5}{8}$.
   C. Felicia ate $\frac{1}{3}$ of a pizza. Linda ate $\frac{1}{6}$ of it.
   D. Lee Yah ate $\frac{5}{12}$ and David ate $\frac{2}{12}$.

7. A. Four students each ate $\frac{1}{2}$ of a muffin. How many muffins did they eat altogether?
   B. Five students each ate $\frac{1}{2}$ of a muffin. How many muffins did they eat altogether?

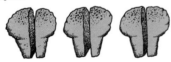

8. A. Eight students each ate $\frac{1}{4}$ of an apple. How many apples did they eat altogether?
   B. Three students each ate $\frac{1}{4}$ of an apple. How many apples did they eat altogether?
   C. Six students each ate $\frac{1}{4}$ of an apple. How many apples did they eat altogether?

Student Guide - page 351

Solving Problems with Pattern Blocks

1. **A.** $\frac{1}{3}$ pizza   **B.** $\frac{1}{4}$ pizza
   C. Table A
   D. $\frac{1}{3}$; There are three students at Table A and 4 students at Table B. Since the pizza at Table A was divided into fewer pieces, each piece is bigger than the 4 pieces at Table B.

2. **A.** $\frac{2}{12}$ pie*   **B.** $\frac{2}{6}$ pie*
   C. $\frac{2}{4}$ pie*
   D. Brandon ate the most pie because his pie was divided into fewer pieces, so each piece is larger.
   E. John

3.* **A.** $\frac{1}{8}$ **B.** $\frac{1}{10}$
   C. One zax is larger than a snark since the whole is divided into fewer pieces to make a zax than to make a snark.

4.* **A.** $\frac{1}{12}, \frac{1}{6}, \frac{1}{4}, \frac{1}{3}, \frac{1}{2}$ **B.** $\frac{2}{12}, \frac{2}{6}, \frac{2}{4}, \frac{2}{3}$
   C. $\frac{1}{10}, \frac{1}{8}, \frac{1}{5}$ **D.** $\frac{3}{10}, \frac{3}{8}, \frac{3}{5}$

5. When the numerators are the same, the fraction with the smaller denominator is the larger fraction.*

6.* **A.** $\frac{1}{2} + \frac{1}{4} = \frac{3}{4}$ pizza
   B. $\frac{3}{8} + \frac{5}{8} = \frac{8}{8}$ or 1 whole pizza
   C. $\frac{1}{3} + \frac{1}{6} = \frac{1}{2}$ pizza
   D. $\frac{5}{12} + \frac{2}{12} = \frac{7}{12}$ pizza

7. **A.** $\frac{1}{2} + \frac{1}{2} + \frac{1}{2} + \frac{1}{2} = 2$ muffins or
   $4 \times \frac{1}{2} = 2$ muffins*
   B. $\frac{1}{2} + \frac{1}{2} + \frac{1}{2} + \frac{1}{2} + \frac{1}{2} = \frac{5}{2}$ or $2\frac{1}{2}$ muffins
   or $5 \times \frac{1}{2} = \frac{5}{2}$ or $2\frac{1}{2}$ muffins

8. **A.** $\frac{1}{4} + \frac{1}{4} + \frac{1}{4} + \frac{1}{4} + \frac{1}{4} + \frac{1}{4} + \frac{1}{4} + \frac{1}{4} = 2$ apples
   or $8 \times \frac{1}{4} = 2$ apples
   B. $\frac{1}{4} + \frac{1}{4} + \frac{1}{4} = \frac{3}{4}$ apple or $3 \times \frac{1}{4} = \frac{3}{4}$ apple
   C. $\frac{1}{4} + \frac{1}{4} + \frac{1}{4} + \frac{1}{4} + \frac{1}{4} + \frac{1}{4} = \frac{6}{4}$ or $1\frac{1}{2}$ apples or
   $6 \times \frac{1}{4} = 1\frac{1}{2}$ apples

*Answers and/or discussion are included in the Lesson Guide.

Student Guide (p. 352)

Homework

1. A. $\frac{3}{12}, \frac{3}{6}, \frac{3}{4}, \frac{3}{3}$

    B. $\frac{3}{10}, \frac{3}{8}, \frac{3}{5}, \frac{3}{4}$

    C. $\frac{1}{8}, \frac{3}{8}, \frac{5}{8}, \frac{8}{8}$

    D. $\frac{1}{12}, \frac{1}{2}, \frac{5}{6}$

2. They ate $\frac{8}{12}$ of the casserole. There is $\frac{4}{12}$ of the casserole left over.

3. A. $\frac{6}{8}$ of the fence

    B. $\frac{2}{8}$ of the fence

4. A. $\frac{3}{4} = \frac{15}{20}$

    B. $\frac{3}{6} = \frac{5}{10}$

    C. $\frac{2}{3} = \frac{6}{9}$

    D. $\frac{3}{8} = \frac{6}{16}$

    E. $\frac{1}{2} = \frac{3}{6}$

    F. $\frac{30}{100} = \frac{3}{10}$

5. A. $\frac{1}{3} + \frac{1}{3} + \frac{1}{3} + \frac{1}{3} = \frac{4}{3}$ or $1\frac{1}{3}$ cookie or $4 \times \frac{1}{3} = \frac{4}{3}$ or $1\frac{1}{3}$ cookie

    B. $\frac{1}{3} + \frac{1}{3} + \frac{1}{3} + \frac{1}{3} + \frac{1}{3} + \frac{1}{3} = 2$ cookies or $6 \times \frac{1}{3} = 2$ cookies

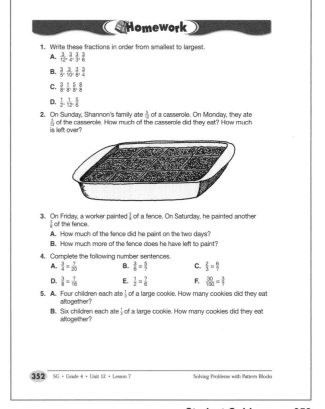

Student Guide - page 352

Lesson 8

Fraction Puzzles

Lesson Overview

Given clues, students work in cooperative groups of four to solve fraction puzzles. After solving the fourth fraction puzzle, students will work independently to explain their solution and to communicate their problem-solving strategies. The Student Rubrics: *Solving* and *Telling* are used as guides for exemplary work.

Key Content

- Representing fractions using pattern blocks and diagrams.
- Working cooperatively to solve problems.
- Solving open-response problems and communicating problem-solving strategies.
- Writing number sentences using fractions.

Homework

1. Assign homework *Questions 1–7* in the *Student Guide.*
2. Assign Home Practice Part 6.

Assessment

1. Puzzle D and the *Puzzle Problem* Assessment Blackline Master provide an assessment of students' problem-solving and communication skills.
2. Use the *Observational Assessment Record* to note students' abilities to solve open-response problems and communicate solution strategies.
3. Transfer appropriate documentation from the Unit 12 *Observational Assessment Record* to students' *Individual Assessment Record Sheets.*

Materials List

Supplies and Copies

Student	Teacher
Supplies for Each Student Group • 1 set of pattern blocks	**Supplies** • envelopes, optional • paper clips, optional
Copies • 1 copy of *Fraction Puzzle Clues* per student group (*Unit Resource Guide* Pages 112–113) • 1 copy of *Puzzle Problem* per student (*Unit Resource Guide* Page 114)	**Copies/Transparencies** • 1 transparency or poster of Student Rubric: *Solving* (*Teacher Implementation Guide,* Assessment section) • 1 transparency or poster of Student Rubric: *Telling* (*Teacher Implementation Guide,* Assessment section) • 1 copy of *TIMS Multidimensional Rubric* (*Teacher Implementation Guide,* Assessment section)

All blackline masters including assessment, transparency, and DPP masters are also on the Teacher Resource CD.

Student Books

Fraction Chart from *Comparing Fractions* (*Student Guide* Page 336)
Fraction Puzzles (*Student Guide* Pages 353–355)
Student Rubrics: *Solving* and *Telling* (*Student Guide* Appendix B, Appendix C, and Inside Back Cover)

Daily Practice and Problems and Home Practice

DPP items S–V (*Unit Resource Guide* Pages 24–26)
Home Practice Part 6 (*Discovery Assignment Book* Page 196)

Note: Classrooms whose pacing differs significantly from the suggested pacing of the units should use the Math Facts Calendar in Section 4 of the *Facts Resource Guide* to ensure students receive the complete math facts program.

Assessment Tools

Observational Assessment Record (*Unit Resource Guide* Pages 13–14)
Individual Assessment Record Sheet (*Teacher Implementation Guide,* Assessment section)
TIMS Multidimensional Rubric (*Teacher Implementation Guide,* Assessment section)

Daily Practice and Problems

Suggestions for using the DPPs are on page 109.

S. Bit: Words to Numbers (URG p. 24)

1. Write the following words as numbers.
   A. two-thirds   B. six-tenths
   C. five-eighths   D. one-twelfth
2. Write the following numbers as words.
   A. $\frac{3}{4}$ B. $\frac{7}{9}$
   C. $\frac{1}{2}$ D. $\frac{2}{5}$

T. Challenge: Art Paper (URG p. 25)

Carlos and Brandon each cut out a rectangle from a piece of drawing paper. Carlos's rectangle was larger—it was $\frac{1}{2}$ of his piece of paper. Brandon's was smaller, but it was $\frac{3}{4}$ of his whole piece.

1. Use *Centimeter Grid Paper* to draw a sketch of Brandon's and Carlos's whole pieces of paper.
2. Shade $\frac{1}{2}$ of Carlos's piece of paper.
3. Shade $\frac{3}{4}$ of Brandon's piece of paper.

U. Bit: Even Products (URG p. 25)

In your journal, explain why all multiples of 4 are even numbers. First, write all the multiples in order from 4 to 40.

V. Challenge: Bank Deposit
(URG p. 26)

The bank gives Maya wrappers so she can roll the coins she saves. Then she deposits the coins. The table shows the value of 1 roll of each type of coin.

Type of Coin	Value of 1 Roll
pennies	50¢
nickels	$2.00
dimes	$5.00
quarters	$10.00

Maya counts her change and puts the coins in wrappers. She has a total of $18.68. What types of coins could she have? How many full rolls of these coins could she have? How many coins would she have left over? List two possible combinations.

Before the Activity

There are four different fraction puzzles and each group should solve all four. The clues for each puzzle are labeled with the same letter of the alphabet and are on the *Fraction Puzzle Clues* Blackline Masters. Make enough copies so each group has a set of clues for each puzzle. Puzzle D is an assessment and students should do it after the other puzzles are completed.

Cut out the clue cards for each puzzle and paper-clip each set of cards together or place the clues for each puzzle in an envelope labeled with the puzzle letter. This will make it easier to hand out and collect the clues.

TIMS Tip

Copy each set of clues on colored paper using a different color for each puzzle letter. After cutting out the clues, laminate them so they can be used over again.

Teaching the Activity

This activity has two parts: Puzzles A, B, and C and the assessment Puzzle D. Students work cooperatively in groups of four for both parts. Then, each student independently writes a full explanation of his or her group's solution and strategies for Puzzle D on a copy of the *Puzzle Problem* Assessment Blackline Master.

Part 1 Fraction Puzzles

Students work in groups of four to solve puzzles using pattern blocks. Each group works together to find a solution they all agree on.

Have students read the vignette on the *Fraction Puzzles* Activity Pages in the *Student Guide*. It introduces the rules for solving the fraction puzzles. Ask students to read the four clues given to Roberto's group and to look at the solutions. *Question 1* asks students to look back at the clues to see if the group's solution satisfies all the guidelines. Students should see that this is an acceptable solution. *Question 2* shows another group's solution to the same puzzle. Since this solution uses only green triangles, it does not meet the guidelines and is not acceptable.

TIMS Tip

Ask students what types of behavior will help their group be successful. Suggested behaviors include:

- Take turns speaking.
- Listen when someone else is talking.
- Respect everyone's ideas.
- Work together.
- Check the group's work for accuracy.
- Talk to the teacher only after the group has been consulted.

Student Guide - page 353

TIMS Tip

This activity works best in groups of four. However, if you have a group of three, have one student read two clues. If you have a group of five, have one student act as the judge for the group, checking the final solution to make sure it meets all the guidelines as specified in the clues. On the next puzzle, switch the role of judge to a different student in the group.

After some work, the students found this solution:

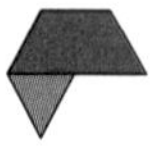

They wrote this number sentence to represent their solution: $\frac{1}{2} + \frac{1}{6} = \frac{2}{3}$.

1. Look back at their clues, and see if this solution fits all the clues they were given.
2. One of the other groups found this solution to the same puzzle.

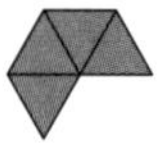

They wrote this number sentence: $\frac{1}{6} + \frac{1}{6} + \frac{1}{6} + \frac{1}{6} = \frac{2}{3}$. Look back at the clues. Does this solution fit all the clues that were given? Why or why not?

Explore

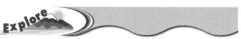

3. Find another solution to this puzzle. Use the clues provided to make sure your solution fits all the clues. Draw a picture of your solution, and write a number sentence to represent your solution.

Homework

Solve the following problems. You may use your fraction chart to help you.

1. Put the following fractions in order from smallest to largest.
   A. $\frac{1}{5}, \frac{1}{9}, \frac{1}{8}, \frac{1}{3}$ **B.** $\frac{3}{10}, \frac{3}{4}, \frac{3}{8}, \frac{3}{5}$ **C.** $\frac{2}{3}, \frac{3}{4}, \frac{5}{8}, \frac{1}{2}$ **D.** $\frac{2}{5}, \frac{3}{8}, \frac{5}{12}, \frac{1}{4}$
2. Put the following fractions in order from smallest to largest.
   A. $\frac{1}{3}, \frac{1}{5}, \frac{1}{2}, \frac{1}{8}$ **B.** $\frac{2}{6}, \frac{2}{4}, \frac{2}{5}, \frac{2}{10}$ **C.** $\frac{4}{5}, \frac{4}{12}, \frac{4}{8}, \frac{4}{6}$ **D.** $\frac{3}{8}, \frac{3}{10}, \frac{3}{5}, \frac{3}{4}$
   E. Explain a strategy for putting fractions in order when the numerators are all the same.

354 SG • Grade 4 • Unit 12 • Lesson 8 Fraction Puzzles

Student Guide* - page 354 *(Answers on p. 115)

TIMS Tip

One strategy for sharing solutions is to combine two groups. As each group finishes, they share their solutions with their partner group before showing it to you or recording it on paper.

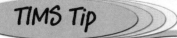

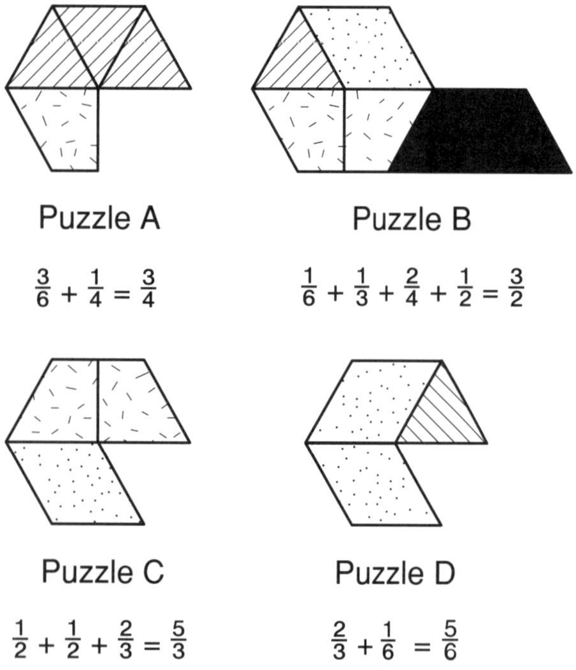
Puzzle A
$\frac{3}{6} + \frac{1}{4} = \frac{3}{4}$
Puzzle B
$\frac{1}{6} + \frac{1}{3} + \frac{2}{4} + \frac{1}{2} = \frac{3}{2}$
Puzzle C
$\frac{1}{2} + \frac{1}{2} + \frac{2}{3} = \frac{5}{3}$
Puzzle D
$\frac{2}{3} + \frac{1}{6} = \frac{5}{6}$

Figure 22: *Some possible solutions for fraction puzzles*

Question 3 asks students to find another solution to this puzzle. Each group should try to find another solution. An additional solution is shown in Figure 21.

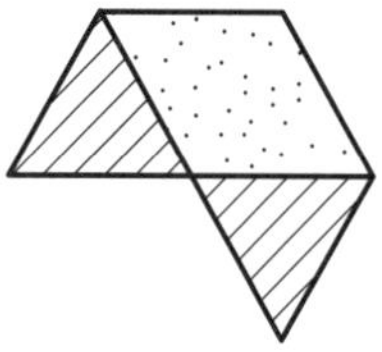

$$\frac{2}{6} + \frac{1}{3} = \frac{2}{3}$$

Figure 21: *Another possible puzzle solution for **Question 3** in the* Student Guide

Students are now ready to solve the first puzzle. Give each group a set of clues for Puzzle A. Each student should receive one clue. Remind students that they can only share their clues with other members of their group by reading the clue aloud.

Once a group has a solution they feel satisfies all the clues, they record their work by tracing the pattern blocks they used onto a sheet of paper. They then write a number sentence to represent their solution. This allows you to check each group's solution at a later time.

Once a group completes a puzzle, you can either collect their clues and give them the clues for the next puzzle or ask them if they can solve the puzzle in another way. Each puzzle has multiple solutions. Accept any solution that fits all the puzzle clues. One possible solution for each is shown in Figure 22.

After a group completes all three puzzles, they proceed to Part 2 of this lesson.

Part 2 Assessment Puzzle

Before students begin writing their solutions, discuss the Student Rubrics: *Solving* and *Telling* to make your expectations clear. Each student should receive one clue for the assessment puzzle (Puzzle D). Remind each student that he or she can only share his or her clue by reading it aloud to the group. Allow time for each group to find a solution to the puzzle.

After finding a solution that all members agree on, students begin the second part of the assessment, which they should complete independently. Each student completes a copy of the *Puzzle Problem* Assessment Blackline Master, which asks students to describe the group's solution and explain the strategies used to solve the problem.

- Assign homework *Questions 1–7* on the *Fraction Puzzles* Activity Pages in the *Student Guide.* These questions review comparing and ordering fractions.

- DPP items S through V all build students' number sense. Bit S asks students to translate between word and symbolic representations of fractions. Challenge T reinforces the fraction concepts of this unit. Bit U addresses even numbers and multiples of 4. Challenge V poses an open-response question involving money.

- Home Practice Part 6 provides an arithmetic review and can provide practice for the Midterm Test in Lesson 9.

Answers for Part 6 of the Home Practice are in the Answer Key at the end of this lesson and at the end of this unit.

---

3. Write a number sentence for each pair of fractions. Use the symbols <, >, or = in each sentence.

   A. $\frac{6}{9}, \frac{3}{4}$ B. $\frac{3}{5}, \frac{3}{8}$ C. $\frac{1}{3}, \frac{3}{8}$

   D. $\frac{1}{2}, \frac{5}{10}$ E. $\frac{4}{5}, \frac{5}{12}$ F. $\frac{3}{9}, \frac{1}{3}$

4. Frank and Jerome each ordered a small cheese pizza for lunch. Frank's pizza was cut into 6 pieces. Jerome's pizza was cut into 8 pieces. Frank ate 2 pieces of his pizza. Jerome ate 3 pieces of his pizza. Which boy ate more pizza? How do you know?

5. Nila and Tanya shared a sandwich for lunch. Nila ate $\frac{1}{2}$ of the sandwich, and Tanya ate $\frac{1}{4}$ of the sandwich. What fraction of the whole sandwich did the two girls eat? Explain how you found your answer.

6. Lee Yah, Luis, John, and Shannon solved a fraction puzzle. Their solution is below. If a yellow hexagon is one whole, write a number sentence for their solution.

7. Frank, Jacob, Irma, and Maya solved a fraction puzzle. Their solution is shown on the right. Does their solution fit the clues? Explain your thinking.

   Clue 1: The red trapezoid is equal to 1 whole.
   Clue 2: Make a shape with a value of $\frac{8}{3}$.
   Clue 3: Use at least two brown trapezoids.
   Clue 4: Do not use any blue rhombuses.

Fraction Puzzles   SG · Grade 4 · Unit 12 · Lesson 8   **355**

Student Guide - page 355 *(Answers on p. 115)*

Name _____   Date _____

PART 6 Arithmetic Review

1. Solve the following problems using mental math or paper and pencil. Estimate to make sure your answers are reasonable.

   A. $231 \times 4 =$ B. $409 \times 5 =$ C. $6283 \times 4 =$ D. $570 \times 5 =$

   E. $46 \times 92 =$ F. $27 \times 44 =$ G. $70 \times 40 =$ H. $83 \times 50 =$

   I. $1092 + 378 =$ J. $3807 - 797 =$ K. $3450 + 4750 =$ L. $8367 - 538 =$

2. Explain your estimation strategy for Question 1C.

3. Solve the following problems.
   A. John's uncle is taking a test to be a cashier at a grocery store. He must show all the ways to give 59¢ in change using exactly 10 coins. Show at least two ways to do this.

   B. The questions on a math test are each worth a certain number of points. Use the table to find the total points if the four questions are answered correctly.

Question	Points Possible
A	$2\frac{1}{2}$
B	$3\frac{1}{4}$
C	5
D	$4\frac{1}{4}$

196 DAB · Grade 4 · Unit 12   EXPLORING FRACTIONS

Discovery Assignment Book - page 196 *(Answers on p. 116)*

- Score the *Puzzle Problem* using the Solving and Telling dimensions of the *TIMS Multidimensional Rubric.* To assist you in scoring students' work using these two dimensions, questions specific to this task follow:

Solving

Did students devise a good plan for solving the problem without assistance from you?

Did students organize their efforts for solving the problem?

Did students stick with the problem until they found a solution acceptable to all group members?

Did students look back at their clues and check their work for accuracy?

Telling

Did students clearly show their solution to this problem using pictures and symbols (a correct number sentence) to clarify their work?

Did students include a complete and clear explanation of their strategies?

Did students support their solution by referring back to the guidelines presented in the clues?

Did students use appropriate fraction names in their explanation?

After students complete their written work, review it and make comments. For example, if students do not use both a picture and a number sentence to show their solutions, suggest that they do so. Students should then revise their work based on your input. After the work is scored, students should add the assessment to their collection folders.

- This activity provides an opportunity to assess students' abilities to solve open-response problems and communicate solution strategies. Record your observations on the *Observational Assessment Record.*

- Transfer appropriate documentation from the Unit 12 *Observational Assessment Record* to the students' *Individual Assessment Record Sheets.*

Extension

Ask groups to find at least two different solutions for each puzzle.

At a Glance

Math Facts and Daily Practice and Problems

DPP Bit S reviews different representations of fractions. Challenge T provides practice with fraction concepts. Bit U reviews multiples and even numbers. Challenge V is a money problem.

Before the Activity

Prepare the clue cards for Fraction Puzzles A–D using the *Puzzle Clues* Blackline Masters.

Part 1. Fraction Puzzles

1. Review class rules for group work.
2. Read the vignette on the *Fraction Puzzles* Activity Pages in the *Student Guide.*
3. Ask students to evaluate the two puzzle solutions in the *Student Guide (Questions 1–2).*
4. Students work in groups to find additional solutions to the same puzzle *(Question 3).*
5. Students work in groups of four to solve the first three fraction puzzles (A–C). They record their solutions by drawing pictures and writing appropriate number sentences.

Part 2. Assessment Puzzle

1. Review the Student Rubrics: *Solving* and *Telling* with students.
2. Pass out a set of clues for Puzzle D to each group.
3. Groups work together to find a solution to the puzzle.
4. Each student works independently to write an explanation of his or her group's solution and a paragraph describing the problem-solving strategies used on the *Puzzle Problem* Assessment Blackline Master.
5. Students revise their work based on your feedback.
6. Score student work using the Solving and the Telling dimensions of the *TIMS Multidimensional Rubric.*
7. Students add their work to their collection folders.

Homework

1. Assign homework *Questions 1–7* in the *Student Guide.*
2. Assign Home Practice Part 6.

Assessment

1. Puzzle D and the *Puzzle Problem* Assessment Blackline Master provide an assessment of students' problem-solving and communication skills.
2. Use the *Observational Assessment Record* to note students' abilities to solve open-response problems and communicate solution strategies.
3. Transfer appropriate documentation from the Unit 12 *Observational Assessment Record* to students' *Individual Assessment Record Sheets.*

Extension

Ask groups to find at least two solutions for each puzzle.

Answer Key is on pages 115–117.

Notes:

Fraction Puzzle Clues

Each group will need one set of puzzle clues for each puzzle. Cut out puzzle clues for Puzzles A–D before class begins. Puzzle D is designed as an assessment and students should use it after the other three puzzles are successfully completed.

✂

PUZZLE A The yellow hexagon equals 1 whole.	PUZZLE A Use 3 or more blocks to make your shape.
PUZZLE A Use at least two different colors of blocks.	PUZZLE A Make a shape with the value of $\frac{3}{4}$.

✂

PUZZLE B Make a shape with the value of $\frac{3}{2}$.	PUZZLE B Use at least 1 blue rhombus.
PUZZLE B The yellow hexagon equals 1 whole.	PUZZLE B Use two brown trapezoids.

✂

PUZZLE C	PUZZLE C
Use no more than 3 blocks.	The red trapezoid equals 1 whole.
PUZZLE C	PUZZLE C
Use at least two blocks.	Make a shape with the value of $\frac{5}{3}$.

✂   Assessment Puzzle Clues

PUZZLE D	PUZZLE D
Make a shape with the value of $\frac{5}{6}$.	The yellow hexagon equals 1 whole.
PUZZLE D	PUZZLE D
Use 3 or 4 blocks.	Use at least 1 green triangle, but not all green triangles.

Puzzle Problem

Work together with your group. Use the four clues to help you build a shape using pattern blocks that meet all the guidelines.

1. Show your group's solution below. Draw a picture and write a number sentence.

2. Write a paragraph explaining the strategies your group used to arrive at this solution.

Student Guide (p. 354)

1. Solution satisfies all guidelines.*

2. Since the figure is made up of all green triangles, the solution does not satisfy the guideline that says, "Use at least 1 green triangle, but not all green triangles."*

3. Another possible solution: $\frac{2}{6} + \frac{1}{3} = \frac{2}{3}$*

Homework

1. **A.** $\frac{1}{9}, \frac{1}{8}, \frac{1}{5}, \frac{1}{3}$ **B.** $\frac{3}{10}, \frac{3}{8}, \frac{3}{5}, \frac{3}{4}$

    C. $\frac{1}{2}, \frac{5}{8}, \frac{2}{3}, \frac{3}{4}$ **D.** $\frac{1}{4}, \frac{3}{8}, \frac{2}{5}, \frac{5}{12}$

2. **A.** $\frac{1}{8}, \frac{1}{5}, \frac{1}{3}, \frac{1}{2}$ **B.** $\frac{2}{10}, \frac{2}{6}, \frac{2}{5}, \frac{2}{4}$

    C. $\frac{4}{12}, \frac{4}{8}, \frac{4}{6}, \frac{4}{5}$ **D.** $\frac{3}{10}, \frac{3}{8}, \frac{3}{5}, \frac{3}{4}$

    E. When the numerators are the same, the smaller fractions have the larger denominators.

Student Guide (p. 355)

3. **A.** $\frac{6}{8} = \frac{3}{4}$

    B. $\frac{3}{5} > \frac{3}{8}$

    C. $\frac{1}{3} < \frac{3}{6}$

    D. $\frac{1}{2} = \frac{5}{10}$

    E. $\frac{4}{5} > \frac{5}{12}$

    F. $\frac{3}{9} = \frac{1}{3}$

4. Jerome ate $\frac{3}{8}$ of his pizza. Frank ate $\frac{2}{6}$ of his pizza. Jerome ate more pizza than Frank. Students may use their fraction charts to compare $\frac{2}{6}$ and $\frac{3}{8}$.

5. $\frac{3}{4}$ of the sandwich. Strategies will vary.

6. $\frac{1}{2} + \frac{1}{6} + \frac{1}{3} = 1$

7. No, they used a blue rhombus.

After some work, the students found this solution:

They wrote this number sentence to represent their solution: $\frac{1}{2} + \frac{1}{6} = \frac{2}{3}$.

1. Look back at their clues, and see if this solution fits all the clues they were given.

2. One of the other groups found this solution to the same puzzle.

They wrote this number sentence: $\frac{1}{8} + \frac{1}{8} + \frac{1}{8} + \frac{1}{8} = \frac{2}{3}$. Look back at the clues. Does this solution fit all the clues that were given? Why or why not?

Explore

3. Find another solution to this puzzle. Use the clues provided to make sure your solution fits all the clues. Draw a picture of your solution, and write a number sentence to represent your solution.

Homework

Solve the following problems. You may use your fraction chart to help you.

1. Put the following fractions in order from smallest to largest.
   A. $\frac{1}{5}, \frac{1}{9}, \frac{1}{8}, \frac{1}{3}$ **B.** $\frac{3}{10}, \frac{3}{4}, \frac{3}{8}, \frac{3}{5}$ **C.** $\frac{2}{3}, \frac{3}{4}, \frac{5}{8}, \frac{1}{2}$ **D.** $\frac{2}{5}, \frac{3}{8}, \frac{5}{12}, \frac{1}{4}$

2. Put the following fractions in order from smallest to largest.
   A. $\frac{1}{3}, \frac{1}{5}, \frac{1}{2}, \frac{1}{8}$ **B.** $\frac{2}{6}, \frac{2}{4}, \frac{2}{5}, \frac{2}{10}$ **C.** $\frac{4}{5}, \frac{4}{12}, \frac{4}{8}, \frac{4}{6}$ **D.** $\frac{3}{8}, \frac{3}{10}, \frac{3}{5}, \frac{3}{4}$

   E. Explain a strategy for putting fractions in order when the numerators are all the same.

Student Guide - page 354

---

3. Write a number sentence for each pair of fractions. Use the symbols <, >, or = in each sentence.
   A. $\frac{6}{8}, \frac{3}{4}$ **B.** $\frac{3}{5}, \frac{3}{8}$ **C.** $\frac{1}{3}, \frac{3}{6}$
   D. $\frac{1}{2}, \frac{5}{10}$ **E.** $\frac{4}{5}, \frac{5}{12}$ **F.** $\frac{3}{9}, \frac{1}{3}$

4. Frank and Jerome each ordered a small cheese pizza for lunch. Frank's pizza was cut into 6 pieces. Jerome's pizza was cut into 8 pieces. Frank ate 2 pieces of his pizza. Jerome ate 3 pieces of his pizza. Which boy ate more pizza? How do you know?

5. Nila and Tanya shared a sandwich for lunch. Nila ate $\frac{1}{2}$ of the sandwich, and Tanya ate $\frac{1}{4}$ of the sandwich. What fraction of the whole sandwich did the two girls eat? Explain how you found your answer.

6. Lee Yah, Luis, John, and Shannon solved a fraction puzzle. Their solution is below. If a yellow hexagon is one whole, write a number sentence for their solution.

7. Frank, Jacob, Irma, and Maya solved a fraction puzzle. Their solution is shown on the right. Does their solution fit the clues? Explain your thinking.

Clue 1: The red trapezoid is equal to 1 whole.
Clue 2: Make a shape with a value of $\frac{3}{2}$.
Clue 3: Use at least two brown trapezoids.
Clue 4: Do not use any blue rhombuses.

Student Guide - page 355

*Answers and/or discussion are included in the Lesson Guide.

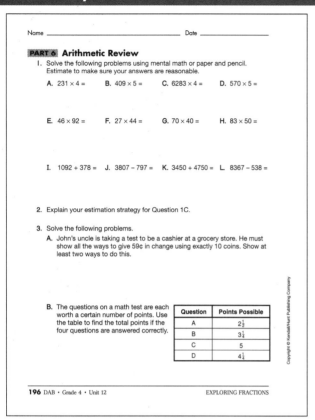

Discovery Assignment Book - page 196

Discovery Assignment Book (p. 196)

Home Practice*

Part 6. Arithmetic Review

1. **A.** 924   **B.** 2045
   C. 25,132   **D.** 2850
   E. 4232   **F.** 1188
   G. 2800   **H.** 4150
   I. 1470   **J.** 3010
   K. 8200   **L.** 7829

2. Possible strategy: $6000 \times 4 = 24{,}000$

3. **A.** Answers will vary. Correct responses include:
   5 dimes + 1 nickel + 4 pennies;
   2 quarters + 9 pennies;
   1 quarter + 4 nickels + 1 dime + 4 pennies

   B. 15 points

Unit Resource Guide (p. 112)

Fraction Puzzle Clues

See Figure 22 in Lesson Guide 8 for answers to Puzzles A–C.†

Unit Resource Guide - page 112

*Answers for all the Home Practice in the *Discovery Assignment Book* are at the end of the unit.
†Answers and/or discussion are included in the Lesson Guide.

Unit Resource Guide (p. 113)

See Figure 22 in Lesson Guide 8 for answers to Puzzles A–C.*

Unit Resource Guide - page 113

Unit Resource Guide (p. 114)

Puzzle Problem

1. Answers will vary. One possible solution to Puzzle D: $\frac{2}{3} + \frac{1}{6} = \frac{5}{6}$

2. Answers will vary.*

Unit Resource Guide - page 114

*Answers and/or discussion are included in the Lesson Guide.

Lesson 9

Midterm Test

Lesson Overview

Students take a paper-and-pencil test consisting of items testing skills and concepts studied in Units 9, 10, 11, and 12.

Key Content

- Assessing concepts and skills.

Math Facts

DPP Bit W is a short quiz on division facts.

Materials List

Supplies and Copies

Student		Teacher	
Supplies for Each Student		**Supplies**	
• calculator • ruler • protractor • base-ten pieces • pattern blocks • 1 fraction chart from Lesson 3			
Copies		**Copies/Transparencies**	
• 1 copy of *Midterm Test* per student (*Unit Resource Guide* Pages 122–126)			

All blackline masters including assessment, transparency, and DPP masters are also on the Teacher Resource CD.

Student Books

Fraction Chart from *Comparing Fractions* (*Student Guide* Page 336)

Daily Practice and Problems and Home Practice

DPP items W–X (*Unit Resource Guide* Page 27)

Note: Classrooms whose pacing differs significantly from the suggested pacing of the units should use the Math Facts Calendar in Section 4 of the *Facts Resource Guide* to ensure students receive the complete math facts program.

Daily Practice and Problems

Suggestions for using the DPPs are on page 120.

W. Bit: Division Quiz: 9s (URG p. 27)

A. $72 \div 9 =$ B. $63 \div 9 =$

C. $54 \div 9 =$ D. $36 \div 9 =$

E. $81 \div 9 =$ F. $45 \div 9 =$

G. $9 \div 9 =$ H. $27 \div 9 =$

I. $18 \div 9 =$

X. Task: Drawing Line Segments
(URG p. 27)

Draw a 5-cm segment on your paper and label the endpoints E and G. Measure and mark the midpoint with the letter F. Extend the line 2 cm past E and label the new endpoint D. Now measure the length of $\overline{DF}$.

Teaching the Assessment

Students take this test individually. It is designed to be completed in one or two class periods. However, you may want to allow more time. Part 1 assesses students' fluency with paper-and-pencil multiplication of one- and two-digit numbers and their estimation skills. Students are to complete this part of the test without a calculator. For Part 2, students will need a ruler, protractor, and a calculator. Base-ten pieces, students' fraction charts, and pattern blocks should also be available.

Remind students to read the directions carefully and to give full explanations of their problem-solving strategies when asked.

Homework and Practice

DPP Task X provides measurement practice that requires understanding of geometric concepts and terminology.

Assessment

- DPP Bit W is a quiz on division facts for the nines.
- The *Midterm Test* assesses skills and concepts studied in Units 9, 10, 11, and 12. Add this test to students' portfolios so you can compare students' performance on this test to their performance on similar activities throughout the year.

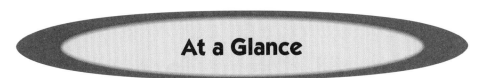

Math Facts and Daily Practice and Problems

DPP Bit W is a short quiz on division facts. DPP Task X provides practice with measuring.

Teaching the Assessment

1. Students complete Part 1 of the test, *Questions 1–9,* without using a calculator.
2. Students complete Part 2 of the test, *Questions 10–25,* using classroom tools, including calculators, rulers, protractors, fraction charts, and pattern blocks.
3. Use DPP Bit W to assess students' fluency with the division facts for the nines.

Answer Key is on pages 127–129.

Notes:

Name _____   Date _____

Midterm Test

Part 1

Use a paper-and-pencil method to complete each of the following problems. Use estimation to check to see if your answer is reasonable.

1. $\begin{array}{r} 73 \\ \times\ 8 \\ \hline \end{array}$

2. $\begin{array}{r} 28 \\ \times\ 23 \\ \hline \end{array}$

3. $\begin{array}{r} 56 \\ \times\ 44 \\ \hline \end{array}$

Use what you know about multiplying by tens to complete the following problems.

4. **A.** $40 \times 10 = $ _____

    B. $40 \times 100 = $ _____

    C. $40 \times 1000 = $ _____

5. **A.** $20 \times 20 = $ _____

    B. $20 \times 200 = $ _____

    C. $20 \times 2000 = $ _____

6. **A.** $50 \times 100 = $ _____

    B. $50 \times 200 = $ _____

    C. $50 \times 300 = $ _____

Estimate the answer to each of the following problems. Write a number sentence to show your thinking. Note: You do not need to find an exact answer.

7. 29×31

8. 48×19

9. 71×21

Part 2

You may use any tool you use in class to complete the remaining problems on this test. For example, you may use a ruler, a protractor, base-ten pieces, or a calculator.

Use the following figure to complete Questions 10–14.

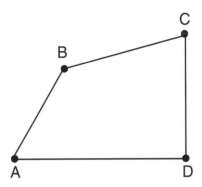

10. Find the measures of the angles.

    ∠A = _____   ∠B = _____

    ∠C = _____   ∠D = _____

11. Name the two rays that form angle C.

12. $\overline{AD}$ is part of what line?

13. **A.** Do any of the lines that form quadrilateral ABCD appear to be parallel?

    B. If so, name the lines.

14. **A.** Do any of the lines that form quadrilateral ABCD appear to be perpendicular?

    B. If so, name the lines.

Use the following figure to complete Questions 15–16.

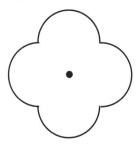

15. **A.** Does this figure have line symmetry?

   B. If so, sketch the lines of symmetry.

16. **A.** Does this figure have turn symmetry?

   B. If so, give the type of turn symmetry.

17. A flat in the base-ten pieces is equal to one whole.

   A. What is the value of a skinny?

   B. What is the value of a bit?

18. A flat in the base-ten pieces is equal to one whole. Write the following numbers using base-ten shorthand.

   A. 2.45   **B.** 17.26   **C.** 23.03

19. A flat is equal to one whole. Write a decimal fraction and a common fraction for each of the following numbers.

Use the following graph to complete Question 20.

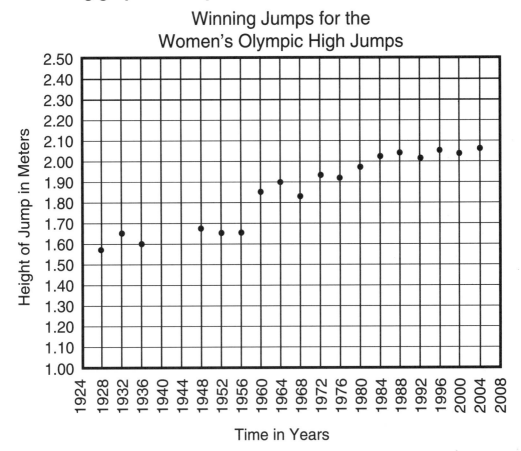

20. A. What was the height of the winning jump in 1960?

B. There were no Olympic Games in 1940 or 1944 during World War II. Predict the height of the winning jump if there had been a high jump contest in 1944.

C. Did you use interpolation or extrapolation to answer 20B? Explain.

Name _____   Date _____

You may use your fraction chart or pattern blocks to help you answer Questions 21–25.

21. If the blue rhombus is one whole,

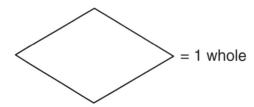

= 1 whole

    A. What fraction is one green triangle?

    B. What fraction is three green triangles?

22. If the green triangle is $\frac{1}{3}$, draw one whole.

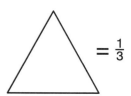

$= \frac{1}{3}$

23. Put the following fractions in order from smallest to largest.
    A. $\frac{3}{10}, \frac{3}{4}, \frac{3}{12}$ **B.** $\frac{1}{4}, \frac{5}{9}, \frac{1}{2}$

24. Complete the following number sentences.
    A. $\frac{2}{3} = \frac{?}{12}$ **B.** $\frac{10}{12} = \frac{5}{?}$ **C.** $\frac{3}{5} = \frac{?}{15}$

25. Michael ate $\frac{3}{8}$ of his apple at lunch time. He ate $\frac{2}{8}$ of his apple after school.

    A. How much of his apple did he eat?

    B. How much of his apple is left?

Assessment Blackline Master

Unit Resource Guide (p. 122)

Midterm Test

Part 1

1. 584
2. 644
3. 2464
4. **A.** 400   **B.** 4000   **C.** 40,000
5. **A.** 400   **B.** 4000   **C.** 40,000
6. **A.** 5000   **B.** 10,000   **C.** 15,000

For Questions 7–9, estimates will vary. One possible estimate is shown.

7. $30 \times 30 = 900$
8. $50 \times 20 = 1000$
9. $70 \times 20 = 1400$

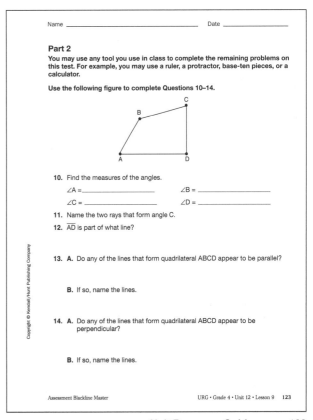

Unit Resource Guide - page 122

Unit Resource Guide (p. 123)

Part 2

10. $\angle A = 60°, \angle B = 135°, \angle C = 75°, \angle D = 90°$
11. $\overrightarrow{CB}$ and $\overrightarrow{CD}$
12. $\overleftrightarrow{AD}$
13. **A.** No.
14. **A.** Yes.
    B. $\overleftrightarrow{CD}$ and $\overleftrightarrow{AD}$

Unit Resource Guide - page 123

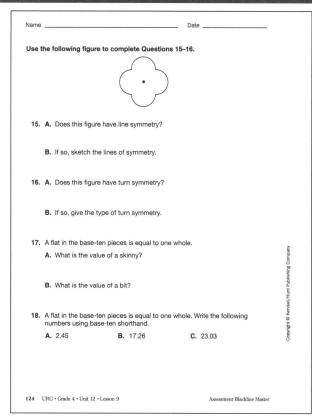

Unit Resource Guide - page 124

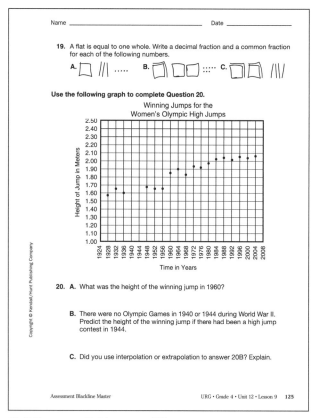

Unit Resource Guide - page 125

Unit Resource Guide (p. 124)

15. A. Yes.

B.

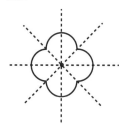

16. A. Yes

B. $\frac{1}{4}$–turn symmetry

17. A. 0.1 or $\frac{1}{10}$

B. 0.01 or $\frac{1}{100}$

18. A. ☐☐ | / | | . . . .

B.

C.

Unit Resource Guide (p. 125)

19. A. 1.35 and $1\frac{35}{100}$

B. 12.08 and $12\frac{8}{100}$

C. 20.4 and $20\frac{4}{10}$

20. A. 1.85 m

B. Answers will vary. About 1.65 m

C. Interpolation. Prediction is between data points.

Unit Resource Guide (p. 126)

21. **A.** $\frac{1}{2}$

    B. $\frac{3}{2}$ or $1\frac{1}{2}$

22.

Note: Arrangements of triangles may vary.

23. **A.** $\frac{3}{12}, \frac{3}{10}, \frac{3}{4}$

    B. $\frac{1}{4}, \frac{1}{2}, \frac{5}{9}$

24. **A.** $\frac{2}{3} = \frac{8}{12}$

    B. $\frac{10}{12} = \frac{5}{6}$

    C. $\frac{3}{5} = \frac{9}{15}$

25. **A.** $\frac{5}{8}$

    B. $\frac{3}{8}$

Name _____ Date _____

You may use your fraction chart or pattern blocks to help you answer Questions 21–25.

21. If the blue rhombus is one whole,

= 1 whole

    A. What fraction is one green triangle?

    B. What fraction is three green triangles?

22. If the green triangle is $\frac{1}{3}$, draw one whole.

$= \frac{1}{3}$

23. Put the following fractions in order from smallest to largest.
    A. $\frac{3}{10}, \frac{3}{4}, \frac{3}{12}$ **B.** $\frac{1}{4}, \frac{5}{9}, \frac{1}{2}$

24. Complete the following number sentences.
    A. $\frac{2}{3} = \frac{?}{12}$ **B.** $\frac{10}{12} = \frac{5}{?}$ **C.** $\frac{3}{5} = \frac{?}{15}$

25. Michael ate $\frac{3}{8}$ of his apple at lunch time. He ate $\frac{2}{8}$ of his apple after school.
    A. How much of his apple did he eat?

    B. How much of his apple is left?

Unit Resource Guide - page 126

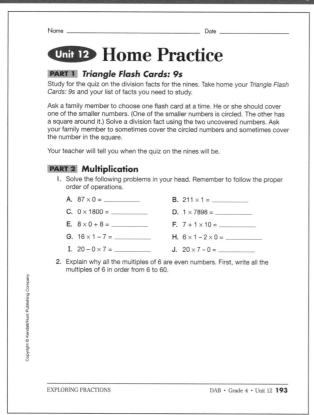

Discovery Assignment Book - page 193

Discovery Assignment Book (p. 193)

Home Practice

Part 2. Multiplication

1. **A.** 0

   B. 211

   C. 0

   D. 7898

   E. 8

   F. 17

   G. 9

   H. 6

   I. 20

   J. 140

2. 6, 12, 18, 24, 30, 36, 42, 48, 54, 60

   An even number has 2 as a factor. Since 2 is a factor of 6, 2 is a factor of all of the multiples of 6. So, all the multiples of 6 are even numbers.

Discovery Assignment Book - page 194

Discovery Assignment Book (p. 194)

Part 3. Fraction Chart

1. **A.** $\frac{2}{12}, \frac{1}{4}, \frac{3}{8}, \frac{2}{3}, \frac{5}{6}$

   B. $\frac{1}{10}, \frac{1}{8}, \frac{4}{9}, \frac{1}{2}, \frac{3}{5}$

2. Answers will vary. Students name 1 or 2 equivalent fractions for each letter.

   A. $\frac{3}{4}, \frac{9}{12}$ **B.** $\frac{1}{3}, \frac{4}{12}$

   C. $\frac{4}{6}, \frac{6}{9}, \frac{8}{12}$ **D.** $\frac{2}{5}$

   E. $\frac{6}{10}$ **F.** $\frac{1}{4}, \frac{2}{8}$

   G. $\frac{1}{2}, \frac{2}{4}, \frac{3}{6}, \frac{4}{8}, \frac{5}{10}$ **H.** $\frac{2}{10}$

3. **A.** $\frac{5}{6} = \frac{10}{12}$

   B. $\frac{8}{10} = \frac{4}{5}$

   C. $\frac{4}{5} = \frac{16}{20}$

4. Answers will vary.

5. Answers will vary.

Discovery Assignment Book (p. 195)

Part 4. Fractions and Decimals

Base-Ten Shorthand	Common Fraction	Decimal Fraction
|/ ⋅⋅⋅⋅	$\frac{25}{100}$ or $\frac{1}{4}$	0.25
◻⋅	$1\frac{1}{100}$	1.01
⋅⋅⋅	$\frac{3}{100}$	0.03
◻◻◻◻◻ /|/||	$5\frac{5}{10}$ or $5\frac{1}{2}$	5.5
/||	$\frac{3}{10}$	0.3
◻◻◻◻/|| ⋅⋅⋅⋅	$4\frac{37}{100}$	4.37
◻◻ ⋅⋅⋅⋅	$2\frac{4}{100}$	2.04
◻◻◻◻/⋅⋅⋅⋅	$4\frac{16}{100}$	4.16
◻/|/|⋅	$10\frac{41}{100}$	10.41

Part 5. A Fraction of a Meter

1. Answers will vary. Possible response: $\frac{6}{10}$ m

2. $\frac{7}{10}$ of a meter

3. Answers will vary. Possible responses: 25 cm or 0.25 m

4. Answers will vary. Possible response: $\frac{1}{10}$ m

5. Answers will vary. Possible response: $\frac{1}{2}$

6. Answers will vary. Possible responses: $1\frac{3}{4}$ or 1.75 meters

7. Answers will vary. Possible response: 2 meters

Name _____ Date _____

PART 4 **Fractions and Decimals**
Complete this table. The flat equals one whole.

Base-Ten Shorthand	Common Fraction	Decimal Fraction
|/ ⋅⋅⋅⋅⋅	$\frac{25}{100}$ or $\frac{1}{4}$	0.25
◻⋅		
		0.03
◻◻◻◻◻ /|/||		
	$\frac{3}{10}$	
		4.37
◻◻ ⋅⋅⋅⋅		
	$4\frac{16}{100}$	
		10.41

PART 5 **A Fraction of a Meter**
Use your fraction chart from Lesson 3, the Fraction Chart in your *Student Guide,* or a meterstick to help you compare fractions.

1. Name a measurement that is greater than $\frac{1}{2}$ meter but less than $\frac{7}{10}$ of a meter.

2. Which is longer: $\frac{7}{10}$ of a meter or 50 centimeters?

3. Name a measurement that is a little less than $\frac{3}{10}$ of a meter.

4. Name a fraction of a meter that is longer than $\frac{5}{100}$ of a meter and shorter than 0.2 meter.

5. Name a fraction that is less than $\frac{7}{10}$ but more than $\frac{1}{5}$.

6. Name a measurement that is longer than 1.54 meters but shorter than $1\frac{9}{10}$ meters.

7. Name a measurement that is more than three times as long as $\frac{1}{2}$ of a meter.

EXPLORING FRACTIONS   DAB • Grade 4 • Unit 12 **195**

Discovery Assignment Book - page 195

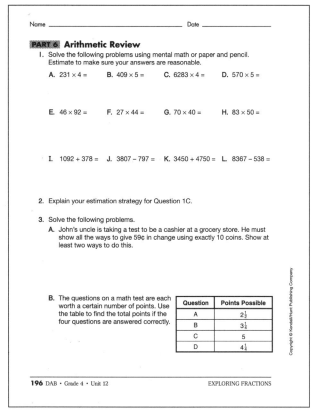

Discovery Assignment Book - page 196

Discovery Assignment Book (p. 196)

Part 6. Arithmetic Review

1. **A.** 924

    B. 2045

    C. 25,132

    D. 2850

    E. 4232

    F. 1188

    G. 2800

    H. 4150

    I. 1470

    J. 3010

    K. 8200

    L. 7829

2. Possible strategy: $6000 \times 4 = 24{,}000$

3. **A.** Answers will vary. Correct responses
    include:

    5 dimes + 1 nickel + 4 pennies;

    2 quarters + 9 pennies;

    1 quarter + 4 nickels + 1 dime + 4 pennies

    B. 15 points

Glossary

This glossary provides definitions of key vocabulary terms in the Grade 4 lessons. Locations of key vocabulary terms in the curriculum are included with each definition. Components Key: URG = *Unit Resource Guide* and SG = *Student Guide.*

A

Acre (URG Unit 6; SG Unit 6)
A measure of land area equal to 43,560 square feet.

Acute Angle (URG Unit 2 & Unit 9; SG Unit 2)
An angle that measures less than 90˚.

All-Partials Algorithm
(URG Unit 7; SG Unit 7)
A paper-and-pencil method for solving multiplication problems. Each partial product is recorded on a separate line. (*See also* partial product.)

$$\begin{array}{r} 186 \\ \times\ 3 \\ \hline 18 \\ 240 \\ 300 \\ \hline 558 \end{array}$$

Angle (URG Unit 2; SG Unit 2)
The amount of turning or the amount of opening between two rays that have the same endpoint.

Angle of Turning (URG Unit 9)
The smallest angle through which a figure can be turned about the center of turning so that the figure coincides with itself.

Area (SG Unit 2)
The area of a shape is the amount of space it covers, measured in square units.

Array (URG Unit 4)
An array is an arrangement of elements into a rectangular pattern of (horizontal) rows and (vertical) columns.

Average (URG Unit 1 & Unit 5; SG Unit 1 & Unit 5)
A number that can be used to represent a typical value in a set of data. (*See also* mean and median.)

B

Base (of an exponent) (SG Unit 4)
When exponents are used, the number being multiplied. In $3^4 = 3 \times 3 \times 3 \times 3 = 81$, the 3 is the base and the 4 is the exponent. The 3 is multiplied by itself 4 times.

Base-Ten Board (URG Unit 3; SG Unit 3)
A tool to help children organize base-ten pieces when they are representing numbers.

Base-Ten Pieces (URG Unit 3; SG Unit 3)
A set of manipulatives used to model our number system as shown in the figure below. Note that a skinny is made of 10 bits, a flat is made of 100 bits, and a pack is made of 1000 bits.

Nickname	Picture	Shorthand
bit		•
skinny		/
flat		
pack		

Base-Ten Shorthand (URG Unit 3; SG Unit 3)
A pictorial representation of the base-ten pieces is shown in Unit 3.

Benchmarks (URG Unit 6; SG Unit 6)
Numbers convenient for comparing and ordering numbers, e.g., $0, \frac{1}{2}, 1$ are convenient benchmarks for comparing and ordering fractions.

Best-Fit Line (URG Unit 5; SG Unit 5)
The line that comes closest to the points on a point graph.

Binning Data (URG Unit 13)
Placing data from a data set with a large number of values or large range into intervals in order to more easily see patterns in the data.

Bit (URG Unit 3 & Unit 6; SG Unit 3)
A cube that measures 1 cm on each edge. It is the smallest of the base-ten pieces and is often used to represent 1. (*See also* base-ten pieces.)

C

Categorical Variable (URG Unit 1; SG Unit 1)
Variables with values that are not numbers. (*See also* variable and value.)

Center of Turning (URG Unit 9; SG Unit 9)
A point on a plane figure around which it is turned. In particular, the point about which an object with turn symmetry is rotated.

Centimeter (SG Unit 10)
A unit of length in the metric system. A centimeter is $\frac{1}{100}$ of a meter.

Certain Event (URG Unit 14; SG Unit 14)
An event that has a probability of 1 (100%).

Common Fraction (URG Unit 10)
Any fraction that is written with a numerator and denominator that are whole numbers. For example, $\frac{3}{4}$ and $\frac{9}{4}$ are both common fractions. (*See also* decimal fraction.)

Commutative Property of Multiplication
(URG Unit 3 & Unit 4)
This is also known as the Order Property of Multiplication. Changing the order of the factors does not change the product. For example, $3 \times 5 = 5 \times 3 = 15$. Using variables, $n \times m = m \times n$.

Composite Number (URG Unit 4)
A number that has more than two distinct factors. For example, 9 has three factors (1, 3, 9) so it is a composite number.

Convenient Number (URG Unit 1 & Unit 7; SG Unit 7)
A number used in computation that is close enough to give a good estimate, but is also easy to compute with mentally, e.g., 25 and 30 are convenient numbers for 27.

Cubic Centimeter (URG Unit 8; SG Unit 8)
The volume of a cube that is one centimeter long on each edge.

D

Decimal (URG Unit 3)
1. A number written using the base-ten place value system.
2. A number containing a decimal point. (*See also* decimal fraction.)

Decimal Fraction (URG Unit 10)
A fraction written as a decimal. For example, 0.75 and 0.4 are decimal fractions and $\frac{75}{100}$ and $\frac{4}{10}$ are called common fractions.

Decimeter (URG Unit 10; SG Unit 10)
A unit of length in the metric system. A decimeter is $\frac{1}{10}$ of a meter.

Degree (URG Unit 2; SG Unit 2)
A degree (°) is a unit of measure for angles. There are 360 degrees in a circle.

Denominator (URG Unit 10 & Unit 12; SG Unit 10 & Unit 12)
The number below the line in a fraction. The denominator indicates the number of equal parts in which the unit whole is divided. For example, the 5 is the denominator in the fraction $\frac{2}{5}$. In this case the unit whole is divided into five equal parts.

Dividend (URG Unit 3; SG Unit 3)
The number that is divided in a division problem, e.g., 12 is the dividend in $12 \div 3 = 4$.

Divisible (URG Unit 7; SG Unit 7)
A number a is divisible by a number b, if there is no remainder when a is divided by b. For example, 12 is divisible by 4 ($12 \div 4 = 3$), but **not** by 5 ($12 \div 5 = 2$ R2).

Division Sentence (SG Unit 3)
A number sentence involving division.

Divisor (URG Unit 3 & Unit 8; SG Unit 3 & Unit 8)
In a division problem, the number by which another number is divided. In the problem $12 \div 4 = 3$, the 4 is the divisor, the 12 is the dividend, and the 3 is the quotient.

E

Edge (URG Unit 9; SG Unit 9)
A line segment where two faces of a three-dimensional figure meet.

Equilateral Triangle (URG Unit 2 & Unit 9; SG Unit 9)
A triangle with all sides and all angles equal.

Equivalent Fractions (URG Unit 12; SG Unit 12)
Fractions that have the same value, e.g., $\frac{2}{4} = \frac{1}{2}$.

Estimate (URG Unit 3, Unit 6, & Unit 7; SG Unit 7)
1. (verb) To find *about* how many.
2. (noun) An approximate number.

Even Number (SG Unit 4)
Numbers that are multiples of 2 (2, 4, 6, 8, etc.) are called even numbers.

Exponent (URG Unit 4; SG Unit 4)
The number of times the base is multiplied by itself. In $3^4 = 3 \times 3 \times 3 \times 3 = 81$, the 3 is the base and the 4 is the exponent. The 3 is multiplied by itself 4 times.

Extrapolation (URG Unit 5; SG Unit 5)
Using patterns in data to make predictions or to estimate values that lie beyond the range of values in the set of data.

F

Face (URG Unit 9; SG Unit 9)
A plane figure that is one side of a three-dimensional figure.

Fact Family (URG Unit 3 & Unit 8; SG Unit 3 & Unit 8)
Related math facts, e.g., $3 \times 4 = 12$, $4 \times 3 = 12$, $12 \div 3 = 4$, $12 \div 4 = 3$.

Factor (URG Unit 3 & Unit 4; SG Unit 3, Unit 4, & Unit 7)
1. In a multiplication problem, the numbers that are multiplied together. In the problem $3 \times 4 = 12$, 3 and 4 are the factors.
2. Whole numbers that can be multiplied together to get a number. That is, numbers that divide a number evenly, e.g., 1, 2, 3, 4, 6, and 12 are all the factors of 12.

Factor Tree (URG Unit 4; SG Unit 4)
A diagram that shows the prime factorization of a number.

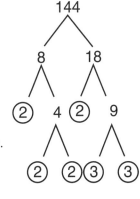

Fair Game or Fair Number Cube (URG Unit 14)
A game in which it is equally likely that any player will win. A number cube is fair if all the faces are equally likely to appear.

Fewest Pieces Rule (URG Unit 3 & Unit 10; SG Unit 3)
Using the least number of base-ten pieces to represent a number. (*See also* base-ten pieces.)

Fixed Variables (URG Unit 1, Unit 2, & Unit 5; SG Unit 5)
Variables in an experiment that are held constant or not changed.

Flat (URG Unit 3 & Unit 6; SG Unit 3)
A block that measures 1 cm $\times$ 10 cm $\times$ 10 cm. It is one of the base-ten pieces and is often used to represent 100. (*See also* base-ten pieces.)

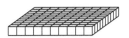

Forgiving Method of Division (URG Unit 13; SG Unit 13)
A paper-and-pencil method for division in which successive partial quotients are chosen and partial products are subtracted from the dividend, until the remainder is less than the divisor. The sum of the partial quotients is the quotient. For example, $644 \div 7$ can be solved as shown at the right. This method of division is called the forgiving method because it "forgives" estimates of the partial quotients that are too low.

```
          92
    7 ) 644
        140  | 20
        ───
        504
        350  | 50
        ───
        154
        140  | 20
        ───
         14
         14  |  2
        ───
          0  | 92
```

Front-End Estimation (URG Unit 3)
Estimation by looking at the left-most digit.

Function (URG Unit 15)
A rule that assigns to any input number exactly one output number. More generally, a rule that assigns to the elements of one set (the domain) exactly one element of another set (the target).

G

H

Hexagon (URG Unit 2)
A six-sided polygon.

Hieroglyphics (URG Unit 11)
An ancient Egyptian form of writing.

I

Identity Property of Multiplication (URG Unit 3)
This is also known as the Property of One for Multiplication. One times any number is that number. Using variables, $n \times 1 = n$.

Impossible Event (URG Unit 14; SG Unit 14)
An event that has a probability of 0 or 0%.

Infinite (URG Unit 9)
Cannot be counted in a finite amount of time. More than any number.

Interpolation (URG Unit 5; SG Unit 5)
Making predictions or estimating values that lie between data points in a set of data.

Intersect (SG Unit 9)
To meet or cross.

J

K

L

Likely Event (URG Unit 14; SG Unit 14)
An event that has a high probability of occurring.

Line (URG Unit 9; SG Unit 9)
A set of points that form a straight path extending infinitely in two directions.

Line Segment (URG Unit 9; SG Unit 9)
A part of a line between and including two points called the endpoints.

Line of Symmetry (URG Unit 9; SG Unit 9)
A line is a line of symmetry for a plane figure if, when the figure is folded along this line, the two parts match exactly.

Line Symmetry (URG Unit 9; SG Unit 9)
A figure has line symmetry if it has at least one line of symmetry.

Liter (SG Unit 8)
Metric unit used to measure volume. A liter is a little more than a quart.

M

Manipulated Variable (URG Unit 5 & Unit 10; SG Unit 5)
In an experiment, the variable with values known at the beginning of the experiment. The experimenter often chooses these values before data is collected. The manipulated variable is often called the independent variable.

Mass (URG Unit 8 & Unit 15; SG Unit 15)
The amount of matter in an object.

Mean (URG Unit 1 & Unit 5; SG Unit 5)
An average of a set of numbers that is found by adding the values of the data and dividing by the number of values.

Measurement Division (URG Unit 4)
Division as equal grouping. The total number of objects and the number of objects in each group are known. The number of groups is the unknown. For example, tulip bulbs come in packages of 8. If 216 bulbs are sold, how many packages are sold?

Measurement Error
The unavoidable error that occurs due to the limitations inherent to any measurement instrument.

Median (URG Unit 1 & Unit 5; SG Unit 1 & Unit 5)
For a set with an odd number of data arranged in order, it is the middle number. For an even number of data arranged in order, it is the number halfway between the two middle numbers.

Megabit (URG Unit 6)
A base-ten model that is a cube with an edge of length 100 cm. It represents 1,000,000 since it has a volume of 1,000,000 cubic cm.

Meniscus (URG Unit 8; SG Unit 8)
The curved surface formed when a liquid creeps up the side of a container (for example, a graduated cylinder).

Meter (SG Unit 10)
A unit of length in the metric system. A meter is a bit more that 39 inches.

Milliliter (ml) (URG Unit 8; SG Unit 8)
A measure of capacity in the metric system that is the volume of a cube that is one centimeter long on each side.

Millimeter (SG Unit 10)
A unit of length in the metric system. A millimeter is one-thousandth of a meter, i.e., one-tenth of a centimeter.

Millions Period (URG Unit 6; SG Unit 6)
The sequence of digits (if any) in the millions place, the ten-millions place, and the hundred millions place. In the number 12,**456,**789,987 the millions period is in bold type.

Multiple (URG Unit 4 & Unit 7; SG Unit 4 & Unit 7)
A number is a multiple of another number if it is evenly divisible by that number. For example, 12 is a multiple of 2 since 2 divides 12 evenly.

Multiplicand (URG Unit 11)
Either of the numbers being multiplied in a multiplication problem.

N

Negative Number (URG Unit 3; SG Unit 3)
A number less than zero; a number to the left of zero on a horizontal number line.

Net (URG Unit 9; SG Unit 9)
A way of representing the surface of a three-dimensional solid in two-dimensions. A net can be obtained by cutting the surface along edges until it can be laid flat on a plane.

Number Sentence
An equation or inequality with numbers. For example, $3 \times 2 + 5 = 10 + 1$ and $2 < 3 + 1$

Numeral (URG Unit 3)
A symbol used to represent a number.

Numerator (URG Unit 10 & Unit 12; SG Unit 10 & Unit 12)
The number written above the line in a fraction. For example, the 2 is the numerator in the fraction $\frac{2}{5}$. (*See also* denominator.)

Numerical Variable (URG Unit 1; SG Unit 1)
Variables with values that are numbers. (*See also* variable and value.)

O

Obtuse Angle (URG Unit 2 & Unit 9; SG Unit 2)
An angle that measures more than 90°.

Odd Number (SG Unit 4)
Numbers that are not multiples of 2 (1, 3, 5 ,7, etc.) are called odd numbers.

Ones Period (URG Unit 6; SG Unit 6)
The sequence of digits (if any) in the ones place, the tens place, and the hundreds place. In the number 12,456,789,**987** the ones period is in bold type.

Operation (SG Unit 7)
A process that takes two numbers and results in a third. This, more precisely, is called a binary operation. For example, addition, subtraction, multiplication, and division are operations.

Order of Operations (URG Unit 7; SG Unit 7)
A convention that determines how to find the value of an expression that has more than one operation.

P

Pack (URG Unit 3; SG Unit 3)
A cube that measures 10 cm on each edge. It is one of the base-ten pieces and is often used to represent 1000. (*See also* base-ten pieces.)

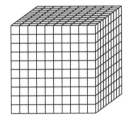

Papyrus (URG Unit 11)
A type of writing paper used by the ancient Egyptians.

Parallel Lines (URG Unit 9; SG Unit 9)
Lines that are in the same direction. In the plane, parallel lines are lines that do not intersect.

Parallelogram (URG Unit 9; SG Unit 9)
A quadrilateral with two pairs of parallel sides.

Partitive Division (URG Unit 4 & Unit 13)
Division as equal sharing. The total number of objects and the number of groups are known. The number of objects in each group is the unknown. For example, Frank has 144 marbles that he divides equally into 6 groups. How many marbles are in each group?

Perimeter (URG Unit 2; SG Unit 2)
The distance around a two-dimensional shape.

Period (URG Unit 6; SG Unit 6)
A group of three places in a large number, starting on the right, often separated by commas as shown at the right.

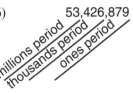

Perpendicular (URG Unit 9; SG Unit 9)
Perpendicular lines are lines that meet at right angles.

Perspective (URG Unit 9)
The art of drawing solid objects on a flat surface so that it produces the same impression as do the actual objects when viewed from a particular point.

Point (URG Unit 9)
An exact position in the plane or in space.

Polygon (URG Unit 9; SG Unit 9)
A two-dimensional connected figure made of line segments in which each endpoint of every side meets with an endpoint of exactly one other side.

Polyhedron (URG Unit 9)
A connected geometric solid whose surface is made of polygons.

Portfolio (URG Unit 2)
A collection of student work that shows how a student's skills, attitudes, and knowledge change over time.

Positive Number (URG Unit 3; SG Unit 3)
A number greater than zero; a number to the right of zero on a horizontal number line.

Powers of Two (URG Unit 6; SG Unit 6)
2 multiplied by itself a certain number of times. $2^1 = 2$, $2^2 = 2 \times 2 = 4$, $2^3 = 2 \times 2 \times 2 = 8$, etc.

Prime Factor (URG Unit 4; SG Unit 4)
A factor of a number that is itself prime.

Prime Number (URG Unit 4; SG Unit 4)
A number that has exactly two factors, itself and 1. For example, 7 has exactly two distinct factors, 1 and 7.

Prism (URG Unit 9; SG Unit 9)
A polyhedron that has two congruent faces, called bases, that are parallel to each other, and all other faces are parallelograms. If the other faces are rectangles the prism is called a right prism.

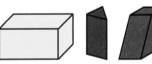

Prisms   Not a prism

Probability (URG Unit 14; SG Unit 14)
A number from 0 to 1 (0% to 100%) that describes how likely an event is to happen. The closer that the probability of an event is to one, the more likely the event will happen.

Product (URG Unit 3; SG Unit 3 & Unit 4)
The answer to a multiplication problem. In the problem $3 \times 4 = 12$, 12 is the product.

Q

Quadrilateral (URG Unit 9; SG Unit 2 & Unit 9)
A polygon with four sides. (*See also* polygon.)

Quick Paper-and-Pencil Method for Addition
(URG Unit 3; SG Unit 3)
A traditional method for
adding multidigit numbers.
See example at right:

$$\begin{array}{r} \overset{1\ \ 1}{1326} \\ +575 \\ \hline 1901 \end{array}$$

Quick Paper-and-Pencil Method for
Subtraction (SG Unit 3)
A traditional method for subtraction.
For example:

$$\begin{array}{r} \overset{0\ 1\ 2\ 1}{\cancel{1237}} \\ -459 \\ \hline 778 \end{array}$$

Quotient (URG Unit 3 & Unit 13; SG Unit 3 & Unit 8)
The answer to a division problem. In the problem
$12 \div 3 = 4$, the 4 is the quotient.

R

Ray (URG Unit 9; SG Unit 9)
A part of a line that has one endpoint and extends
indefinitely in one direction.

Recording Sheet (URG Unit 3; SG Unit 3)
A place value chart used for addition and subtraction
problems.

Rectangle (URG Unit 2 & Unit 9)
A quadrilateral with four right angles.

Reflex Angle (URG Unit 2)
An angle larger than 180° but less than 360°.

Regular (URG Unit 9)
A polygon is regular if all sides are of equal length and
all angles are equal.

Remainder (URG Unit 13)
Something that remains or is left after a whole number
division problem. The portion of the dividend that is not
evenly divisible by the divisor, e.g., $16 \div 5 = 3$ with
1 as a remainder.

Responding Variable (URG Unit 5 & Unit 10;
SG Unit 5)
The variable whose values result from the experiment.
Experimenters find the values of the responding variable
by doing the experiment. The responding variable is often
called the dependent variable.

Rhombus (URG Unit 2)
A quadrilateral with four sides of equal length.

Right Angle (URG Unit 2 & Unit 9; SG Unit 2)
An angle that measures 90°.

Roman Numeral (URG Unit 3; SG Unit 3)
A system of representing numbers used by the
Romans. The symbol I represents 1, V represents
five, X represents ten, etc.

Rounded Number (URG Unit 6 & Unit 7)
See rounding.

Rounding (URG Unit 6)
Replacing a number with the nearest convenient number.
Numbers are often rounded to the nearest whole number,
ten, hundred, fifty, etc.

S

Skinny (URG Unit 3 & Unit 6; SG Unit 3)
A block that measures 1 cm × 1 cm
× 10 cm. It is one of the base-ten
pieces that is often used to represent 10.
(*See also* base-ten pieces.)

Solid (URG Unit 9; SG Unit 9)
A three-dimensional figure that has volume greater
than 0.

Square (URG Unit 2)
A polygon with four equal sides and four right angles.

Square Inch (SG Unit 2)
The area of a square with a side length of one inch.

Square Number (URG Unit 4; SG Unit 4)
A number that is the result of multiplying a whole
number by itself. For example, 36 is a square number
since $36 = 6 \times 6$.

Square Root (URG Unit 15)
The square root of a number N is the number whose square
is N. The symbol for square root is $\sqrt{\ }$. For example,
the square root of 25 is 5, since $5 \times 5 = 25$. In symbols
we write $\sqrt{25} = 5$. The square root of 26 is not a whole
number.

Subtractive Principle (URG Unit 3; SG Unit 3)
A method of interpreting certain Roman numerals.
For example, IX represents 9 while XI represents 11.

Super Bit (URG Unit 6)
A base-ten model that is a cube with an edge of length
10 cm. It represents 1,000 since it has a volume of 1,000
cubic centimeters. It is usually called a pack.

Super Flat (URG Unit 6)
A base-ten model that is a rectangular solid that measures
10 cm × 100 cm × 100 cm. It represents 100,000 since
it has a volume of 100,000 cubic cm.

Super Skinny (URG Unit 6)
A base-ten model that is a rectangular solid that measures
10 cm × 10 cm × 100 cm. It represents 10,000 since it
has a volume of 10,000 cubic cm.

Survey (SG Unit 13)

An investigation conducted by collecting data from a sample of a population and then analyzing it. Usually surveys are used to make predictions about the entire population.

T

Tally

A way of recording a count by making marks. Usually tallies are grouped in fives.

Ten Percent (10%) (URG Unit 6 & Unit 7)

10 out of every hundred or $\frac{1}{10}$.

Thousands Period (URG Unit 6; SG Unit 6)

The sequence of digits (if any) in the thousands place, the ten-thousands place, and the hundred-thousands place. In the number 12,456,**789,**987 the thousands period is in bold type.

TIMS Laboratory Method (URG Unit 1; SG Unit 1)

A method that students use to organize experiments and investigations. It involves four phases: draw, collect, graph, and explore. It is a way to help students learn about the scientific method.

Translational Symmetry (URG Unit 9)

A pattern has translational symmetry if there is a translation that moves the pattern so it coincides with itself.

Trapezoid (URG Unit 2)

A quadrilateral with exactly one pair of parallel sides.

Triangle (URG Unit 2)

A polygon with three sides.

Turn-Around Facts (URG Unit 3; SG Unit 3)

Multiplication facts that have the same factors but in a different order, e.g., $3 \times 4 = 12$ and $4 \times 3 = 12$. (*See also* commutative property of multiplication.)

Turn-Around Rule (URG Unit 4)

A term used to describe the commutative property of multiplication. (*See also* commutative property of multiplication.)

Turn Symmetry (URG Unit 9; SG Unit 9)

A figure has turn symmetry if it can be rotated around a point (called the center of turning) through an angle less than 360° and so that the turned figure matches the original.

Type of Turn Symmetry (URG Unit 9)

The number of times a figure coincides with itself when it is rotated about its center of turning. For example, a square has 4-fold turn symmetry. This is also called $\frac{1}{4}$ turn symmetry.

U

Undefined (Division by Zero) (URG Unit 13; SG Unit 13)

We say division by 0 is undefined because there is no number that satisfies the definition of division when 0 is the divisor. For example, if there were a number $N = 3 \div 0$, it would be the unique number N that makes $N \times 0 = 3$ a true statement. There is no such N.

Unlikely Event (URG Unit 14; SG Unit 14)

An event that has small probability.

V

Value (URG Unit 1; SG Unit 1)

The possible outcomes of a variable. For example, red, green, and blue are possible values for the variable *color*. Two meters and 1.65 meters are possible values for the variable *length*.

Variable (URG Unit 1; SG Unit 1)

1. An attribute or quantity that changes or varies. (*See also* categorical variable and numerical variable.)
2. A symbol that can stand for a variable.

Vertex (URG Unit 2 & Unit 9; SG Unit 2 & Unit 9)

The common endpoint of two rays or line segments.

Volume (URG Unit 8 & Unit 9; SG Unit 8)

The measure of the amount of space occupied by an object.

Volume by Displacement (SG Unit 8)

A way of measuring volume by measuring the amount of water (or some other fluid) it displaces.

W

Weight (URG Unit 15; SG Unit 15)

A measure of the pull of gravity on an object. One unit for measuring weight is the pound.

X

Y

Z

Zero Property of Multiplication (URG Unit 3)

Any number times zero is zero. Using variables, $n \times 0 = 0$.